The
Service
Propers
Noted

The Service Propers Noted

THE INTROITS AND INTERVENIENT CHANTS
FOR THE SUNDAYS, FEASTS, AND OCCASIONS
OF THE LITURGICAL YEAR SET TO
FORMULARY TONES

prepared by
Paul Bunjes

*Authorized by the Commission on Worship,
Liturgics, and Hymnology of The Lutheran
Church — Missouri Synod*

CONCORDIA PUBLISHING HOUSE
ST. LOUIS, MISSOURI

COPYRIGHT 1960 BY
CONCORDIA PUBLISHING HOUSE
SAINT LOUIS, MISSOURI
INTERNATIONAL COPYRIGHT SECURED
ALL RIGHTS RESERVED

NOTICE

The Formulary Tones, both in melody and in harmony, together with the pointing of the texts, are covered by the above copyrights. The copying, either of separate parts or the whole of this work, by any process whatsoever, whether for private use, for profit, or for any other purpose, is forbidden by law and subject to the penalties prescribed by Section 28 of the Copyright Law in force July 1, 1909.

Choir Edition, No. 97-7598 Paper cover
  No. 97-7600 Cloth cover

Made in the United States of America

Foreword

VARIOUS REASONS prompted the *Commission on Worship, Liturgics, and Hymnology* of *The Lutheran Church — Missouri Synod* to endorse heartily the publication of the present volume. In the years 1942 and 1944 respectively this commission made available through Concordia Publishing House *The Introits for the Church Year* and *The Graduals for the Church Year*. However, already then the intent of the commission was to make available additional settings of the Introits, Graduals, and other liturgical materials. Although smaller and more limited collections of such settings have been made available by Concordia during the interim, Prof. Bunjes' present opus is the largest and the only complete collection of Introits and Graduals released since 1942 and 1944 by Concordia Publishing House.

A distinctive feature of the settings found in the present volume is that they are genuine chant settings written for English texts. The eight Gregorian psalm tones (used in *The Introits for the Church Year*, 1942) were originally composed for Latin texts and therefore are not always well suited for English texts. Anglican chant (used in *The Graduals for the Church Year*, 1944) is not ideal chant, since it is in large part melodic and harmonic. Also it is dated and is falling into disuse. The Formulary Tones, though related to plainsong and, in part, to chorale melodies, are nevertheless genuine chant which take into consideration the intrinsic and distinctive character of the English language. Since they are related to music that is familiar, they will not sound strange or dated. On the other hand, the elements of originality, freshness, and vigor are not lacking.

Making these settings of the Introits and Graduals of the church year available indicates that, though rooted in the traditions of the past, we of the church accommodate ourselves to the best standards and practices of the present. Although the extremes of much musical modernity have not been employed in these Formulary Tones, yet they are creations of the present. They were written for the church of the 20th century and hence become a part of the rich musical heritage of the church. It is our hope that they will enjoy widespread use and help to pave the way for the creation of further materials for the services of corporate worship of the church.

    WALTER E. BUSZIN, Chairman
    The Commission on Worship,
      Liturgics, and Hymnology
      of *The Lutheran Church —*
        Missouri Synod

August 2, 1960

In our day the music of the Liturgy, both in Catholic and Protestant churches, is in a state of flux. One of the real problems confronting our scholars has been how to give musical expression to the liturgical texts of the service, such as Introits, Graduals, Tracts, and Alleluias.

Martin Luther faced the same problem when he found it necessary to produce his *Deutsche Messe*. With the deep insight of a genius, he used the ancient melodies of the church for his German mass, but he gave them German forms. He felt that the melodies, wedded to a Latin text, could not be fitted to a German translation. He said: "Both texts and notes, accent and manner, must come out of the vernacular *(Muttersprache)* otherwise it is all an imitation, as the monkeys do."

Since Luther's day many attempts have been made both in Europe and in America to fit the German and English texts to the ancient Latin melodies. We know today that most of these attempts were not creative, but experimental and artificial. They show a regrettable lack of understanding of the principles underlying the ancient liturgy, which grew organically into a great work of art, and has a history of service to the church of more than 1500 years.

The author of this volume has given the problem many years of intensive study. His approach to the question of English chant is, in my opinion, the only correct answer to the problem: *Create new melodies, designed to carry the English text as perfectly as possible in its rhythm and inflection.*

I wish this volume well. It is a fitting and important contribution to the musical heritage of the church.

Theo. Hoelty-Nickel

Valparaiso University
July 1960

Preface

The Service Propers Noted presents the Introits and Intervenient Chants of the service for the entire church year including the minor festivals. It is a foundational service book for use by choirs, in which the texts are set to the Formulary Tones. Two editions are provided: the present one, a choir edition, containing all of the melodies and texts needed by the choir; a second one, an accompanimental edition, containing the full accompaniments for organ. In both editions the tunes and texts are printed out note for note, and the volumes agree perfectly with one another.

The Formulary Tones

The Formulary Tones,* which provide the musical vehicle for the texts of the service propers, are twelve in number. Each one is cast into one of the church modes. The melodies are entirely new, being designed to carry the English text perfectly with respect to its rhythm and inflection. In a number of instances, quotations from the great chorale melodies of the church have been incorporated into the tones.

Following is an example of Formulary Tone I, showing the seven identifiable parts of it:

1. The intonation. 2. The reciting tone. 3. The ante-medial inflection. 4. The medial cadence. 5. The second reciting tone. 6. The ante-terminal pause. 7. The terminal cadence.

In addition, two interpretative signs appear in this book. They are: a. the *signum cadentiae,* b. the *signum accentus.*

The intonation is used to begin a chant or any of its formal sections; it is not used within a section. The reciting tone carries the first phrase of the verse and leads directly into the medial cadence. The second reciting tone carries the second phrase of the verse and leads into the terminal cadence which closes the verse. The ante-medial inflection occurs only when the first half-verse requires division, and the ante-terminal pause only when the second half-verse needs to be divided. The *signum cadentiae* appears in the text and reminds the singer where the cadence begins. The *signum accentus,* placed over a note, reminds the singer that this note must be stressed.

Supplements

Each tone is provided with a supplementary set of alleluias, laid out in four parts. These are used in some of the Introits and Intervenient Chants. They may be performed in unison with organ, or in parts with organ, or *a cappella.*

* A complete explanatory monograph, discussing the Formulary Tones in detail, is projected by the publisher. It will be entitled, *The Formulary Tones Annotated.*

Following are the alleluias for Formulary Tone I:

Each tone also presents a special version of itself for use with the Gloria Patri of the Introit. The melody is an elaborated form of the simple tone. The Gloria Patri for Formulary Tone I is as follows:

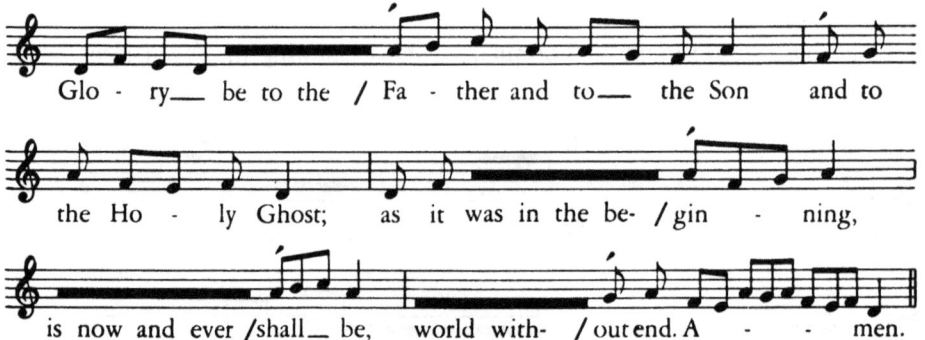

Performance

While learning and performing the chants, the singers should strive to express the text, projecting both thought and mood as intelligently and meaningfully as possible. Should the thought of a chant exhibit a mood of rejoicing, let it be sung with full heart and voice; should it be penitential in character, let the manner of performance reflect this mood. The singer's function is to relate the thought of the text and the mood of the music in an effective and expressive way.

Singing the Chants

Ordinarily, a normal, confident singing voice should carry the text. Let it be sung as one would speak it: clearly, well-modulated, forward-moving, and of adequate strength to make it easy to understand and satisfying to hear. A perfect unison tone must be diligently cultivated by all singers. All syllables of the text must be articulated cleanly at the same time and on the same pitch. The entire group must feel and express the text as one, and strive for an effortless, flowing motion and rendition. The notes of the chant have no determinate time values, the melodies no fixed meters; hence, the movement of the spoken text must take the melodies and shape them to conform to its own motions.

The intonation and the beginning of each subsequent verse should reflect confidence and singleness of purpose. The general movement should be directly and firmly established here. Let the general disposition of the on-going text propel the motion forward. Avoid extremes; there should, for example, be no perceptible change in this respect between the plane of the recitation and the melodic curve of the cadence. A breath should be taken at each bar line, half, single, or double, to help articulate the thought of the text, and to refresh the voice.

Rhythm of the Chants

The normal speech rhythm is the controlling rhythm of the chant, establishing the grouping of the syllables. Speak the text in an exemplary, declamatory way before allowing the chant melody to carry it. An equal pulsation of the syllables would be wooden and deadly; rather, let the subtle grouping of the text syllables be the governing force of the musical rhythm.

Organizing the Chants

The chants of the service should most often be performed directly; i. e., by one soloist or by one group clear through. Occasionally responsorial or antiphonal organization may be used to relieve the monotony of direct chant. Responsorial organization may be applied to the Introit, where the chorus sings the antiphons and Gloria Patri, while a soloist sings the *psalmellus*. The Greater Alleluia lends itself to antiphonal organization: both choirs sing the introductory alleluias, Chorus I the *versus,* Chorus II the alleluia, Chorus I the *versus,* and both choirs the closing alleluias.

Accompaniment

The accompaniment of the chant should support the singing but not envelop it. Light eight- and four-foot stops, without pedal, lend themselves well, giving the choir a clear delineation of the pitch without suppressing the voices. The accompaniment edition contains all of the accompaniments printed out in full.

Following is the accompaniment for Formulary Tone I:

Acknowledgments

The writer wishes to express gratitude to his colleagues, and in particular to Thomas Gieschen for invaluable assistance in the detailed preparation of the Formulary Tones, and for his consistent encouragement of the project. The preparation of the manuscript for this volume was undertaken by Ruth Pralle and George Krieger, to whom my thanks are herewith expressed.

During the formative stages of this project a number of church choirs of various size and ability and from different parts of the country gave generously of their time and talent to test the different tones and chants in their services. Many valuable suggestions were received and incorporated into the overall plan. Such assistance was much appreciated and is hereby acknowledged.

Paul G. Bunjes

July 13, 1960
Melrose Park, Illinois

*The Introits
and
Intervenient Chants
for the
Sundays and Feasts
of the
Liturgical Year*

The First Sunday in Advent

1. The complete form of the Introit is presented here as a model for the Advent season. 2. Antiphon 3. Psalmellus 4. Gloria Patri

The Intervenient Chants — Formulary Tone II

The Gradual

R.[1] All they that / wait on Thee shall not be a-/ sham-ed O Lord.

V.[2] Show me Thy / ways, O Lord, teach me Thy paths.

The Alleluia [3]

I-II.[4] Al - le - lu - ia! Al - le - lu - ia!

V.[2] Show us Thy / mer-cy, O Lord, and grant us / Thy sal-va-tion.

II.[4] Al - le - lu - ia!

1. Responsorium 2. Versus 3. The Alleluia is to be sung immediately upon the conclusion of the Gradual. 4. The jubilant Alleluias should, if at all possible, be sung in four parts (SATB); if not, the upper part may be sung in unison by the whole choir, or by an antiphonal junior or children's choir.

The Second Sunday in Advent

The Introit — *Formulary Tone I*

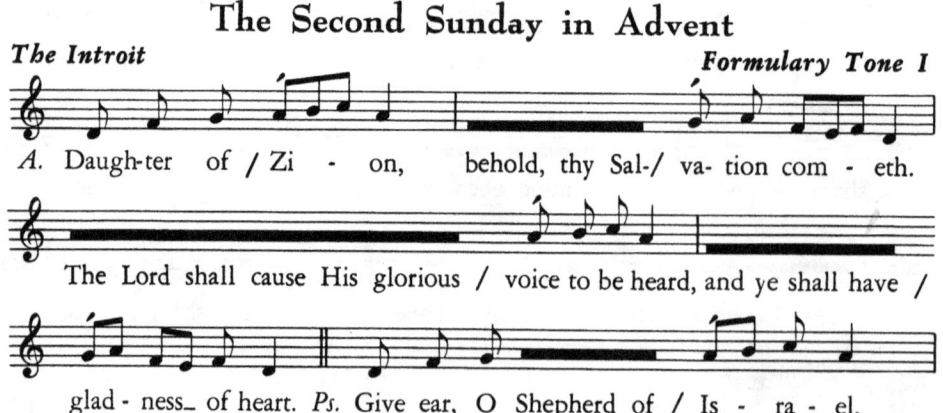

A. Daugh-ter of / Zi - on, behold, thy Sal-/ va-tion com-eth.

The Lord shall cause His glorious / voice to be heard, and ye shall have /

glad-ness of heart. *Ps.* Give ear, O Shepherd of / Is - ra-el,

Thou that leadest / Jo-seph like — a flock. *Gloria Patri I p. 9 / Repeat Antiphon*

The Intervenient Chants — *Formulary Tone II*

The Gradual

R. Out — of Zion, the perfection of beauty, / God hath shin-ed; our / God shall come. V. Gather My saints to-/ geth-er un-to Me: those that have made a covenant with / Me by sac-ri-fice.

The Alleluia

I-II. Al-le-lu-ia! Al-le-lu-ia!

V. The — powers of heaven / shall be shak-en; and then shall they see the Son of Man coming in a cloud with / pow'r and great glo-ry.

II. Al-le-lu-ia!

The Third Sunday in Advent

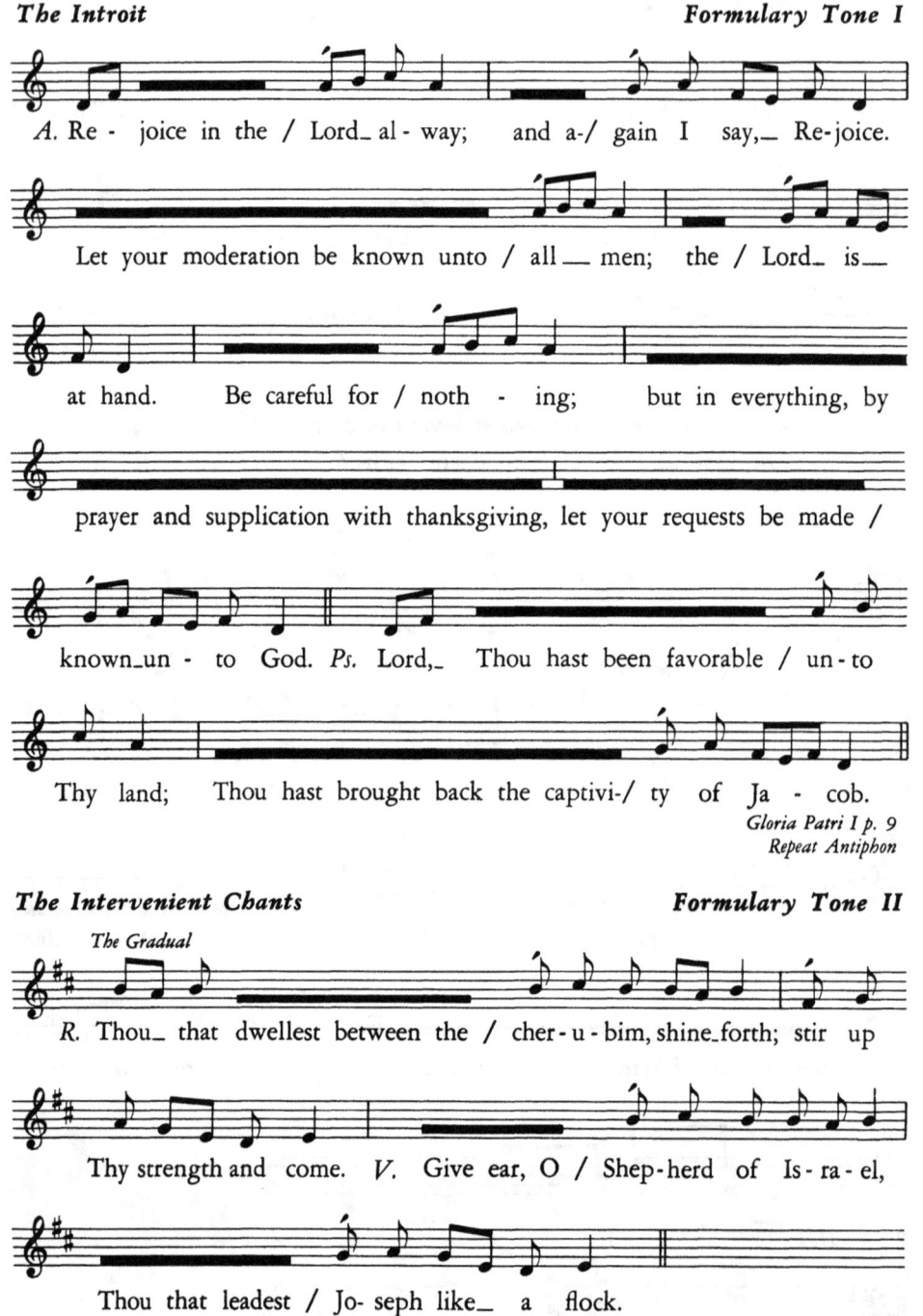

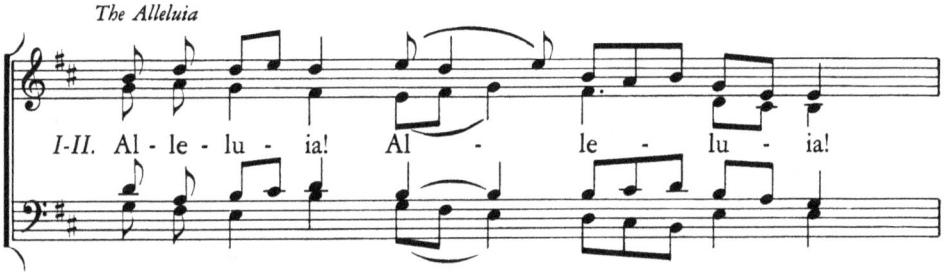

The Alleluia

I-II. Al-le-lu-ia! Al-le-lu-ia!

V. Stir up / Thy strength, and / come and save us.

II. Al-le-lu-ia!

The Fourth Sunday in Advent

The Introit   *Formulary Tone I*

A. Drop down, ye heavens, / from a-bove, and let the / skies pour down right-eous-ness. Let the earth / o-pen and bring / forth sal-va-tion.

Ps. The heavens declare the / glo-ry of God, and the firmament / show-eth His hand-i-work.

Gloria Patri I p. 9
Repeat Antiphon

The Intervenient Chants *Formulary Tone II*

The Gradual

The Alleluia

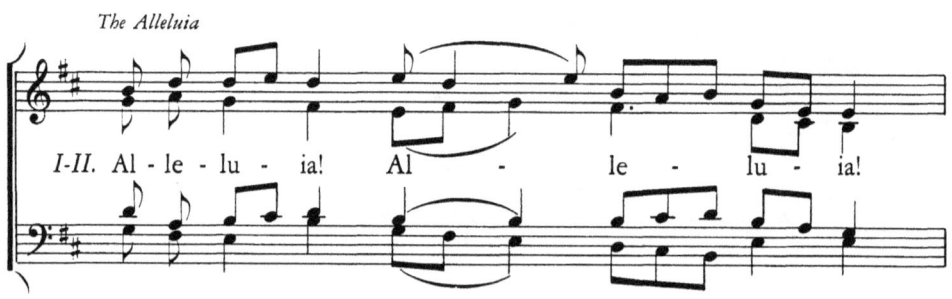

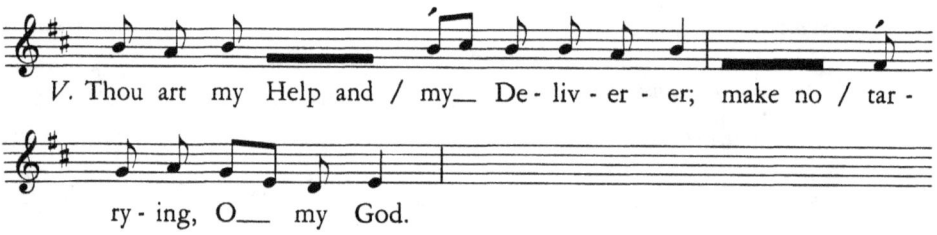

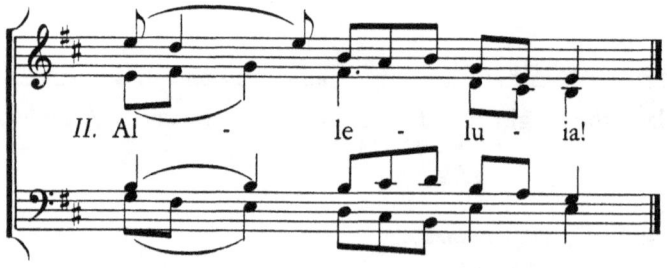

I

The Gloria Patri for the Advent Season Introits

Christmas Day, the Feast of the Nativity of Our Lord

The Introit[1] *Formulary Tone XI*

A.[2] Un-to us a / Child is born, unto us a Son is / giv - -en;

and the government shall / be up-on His shoul - der

And His name shall be called Wonderful, Counselor, the / Might -y

God, the Everlasting / Fa-ther, the Prince of Peace. Ps.[3] Oh, sing unto

the /Lord a new song, for / He hath done mar - - -v'lous things.

G.[4] Glo - ry be to the / Fa -ther and to the Son and to the Ho-ly Ghost;

as it was in the be-/ gin - ning, is now, and / ev-er shall be,

world with-/ out end. A - - - - men. A.[2] Un-to us a / Child is born,

unto us a Son is / giv - en; and the government shall / be up-on

His shoul -der. And His name shall be called Wonderful, Counselor,

the /Might-y God the Everlasting / Fa -ther, the Prince of Peace.

1. The complete form of the Introit is presented here as a model for the Christmas Cycle. 2. Antiphon. 3. Psalmellus. 4. Gloria Patri.

V.² The Lord / said unto Me: Thou art My Son, this / day have I be-got-ten Thee.

II.⁴ Alleluia! Alleluia! Alleluia!

1. Responsorium. 2. Versus. 3. The Alleluia is to be sung immediately upon the conclusion of the Gradual. 4. The jubilant Alleluias should, if at all possible, be sung in four parts (SATB); if not, the upper part may be sung in unison by the whole choir, or by an antiphonal junior or children's choir.

The Intervenient Chants (alternate) — Formulary Tone XII

The Gradual

R. All the ends of the earth have seen the sal-/ va-tion of our God; make a joyful noise unto the / Lord, all the earth. V. The Lord hath made / known His sal-va-tion; His righteousness hath He openly showed in the / sight of the hea-then.

The Alleluia

I-II. Alleluia! Alleluia! Alleluia! Alleluia!

V. Oh, come, let us / sing un-to the Lord; let us worship and / bow down be - fore Him.

Al - le - lu - - - - - ia!
II. Al - - le lu - - - - - ia!
Al - le - lu - - - - - ia!

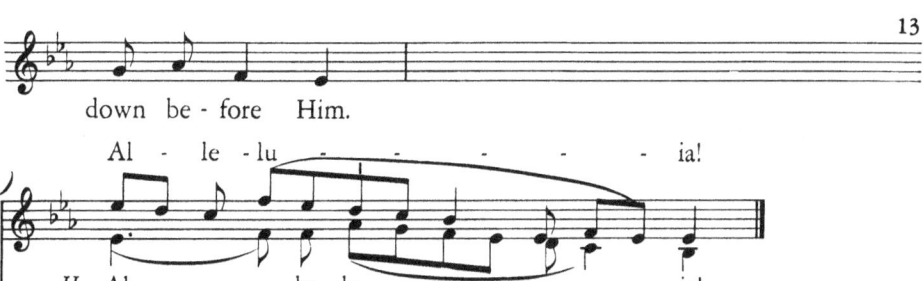

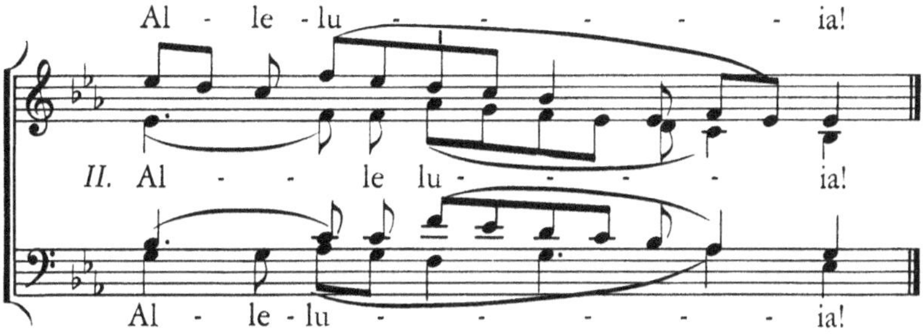

The Second Christmas Day

The Introit ***Formulary Tone XI***

(The Introit, or its alternate, is the same as for Christmas Day, the Feast of the Nativity of Our Lord, p. 10)

The Intervenient Chants ***Formulary Tone XII***

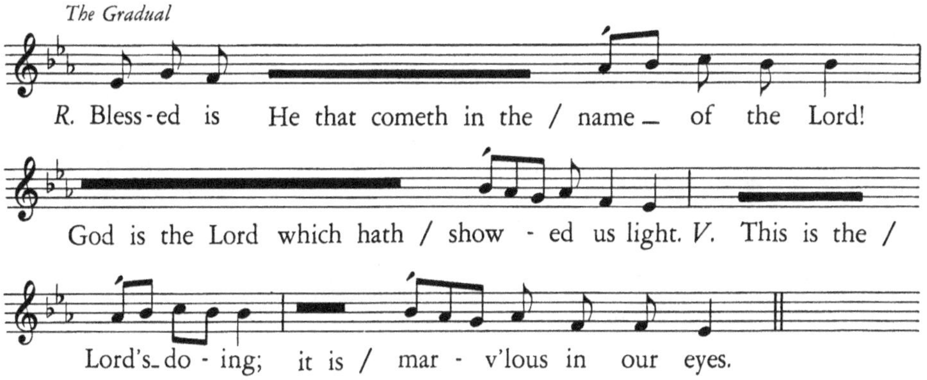
The Gradual
R. Bless-ed is He that cometh in the / name_ of the Lord!
God is the Lord which hath / show - ed us light. V. This is the /
Lord's_do - ing; it is / mar - v'lous in our eyes.

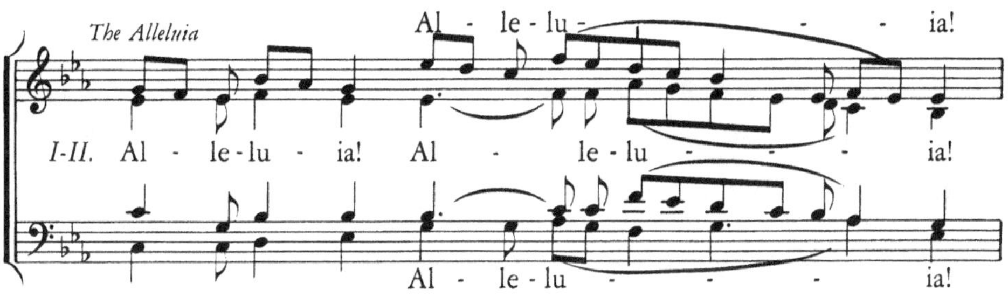
The Alleluia
Al - le - lu - - - ia!
I-II. Al - le - lu - ia! Al - le - lu - - - ia!
Al - le - lu - - - ia!

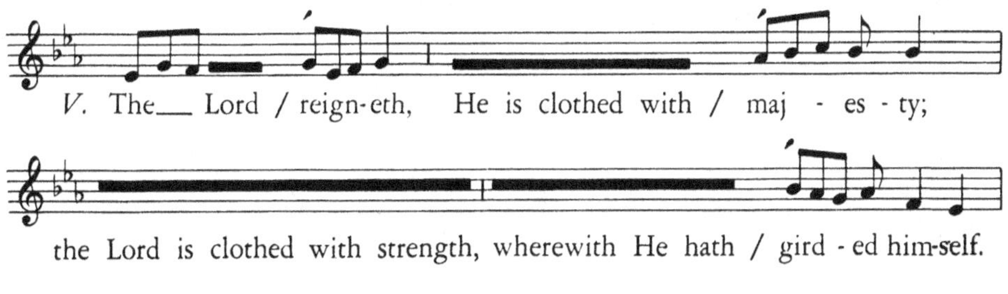
V. The_ Lord / reign-eth, He is clothed with / maj - es - ty;
the Lord is clothed with strength, wherewith He hath / gird - ed him-self.

Al - le- lu - - - - ia!
II. Al - - le - lu - - - - - ia!
Al - le - lu - - - - ia!

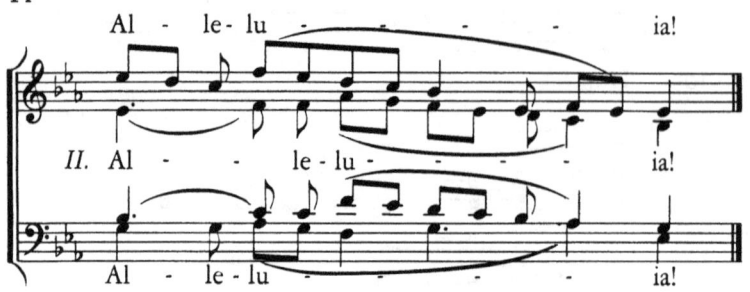

The Sunday After Christmas

The Introit ***Formulary Tone XI***

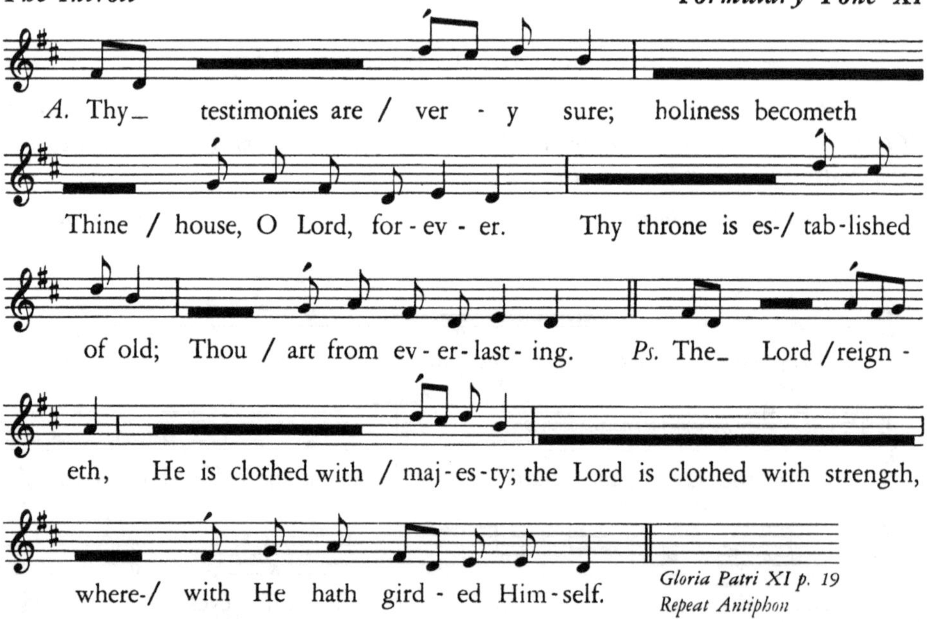
A. Thy_ testimonies are / ver - y sure; holiness becometh
Thine / house, O Lord, for - ev - er. Thy throne is es-/ tab-lished
of old; Thou / art from ev - er - last - ing. Ps. The_ Lord /reign -
eth, He is clothed with / maj - es - ty; the Lord is clothed with strength,
where-/ with He hath gird - ed Him - self.
Gloria Patri XI p. 19
Repeat Antiphon

The Introit (alternate) ***Formulary Tone XI***

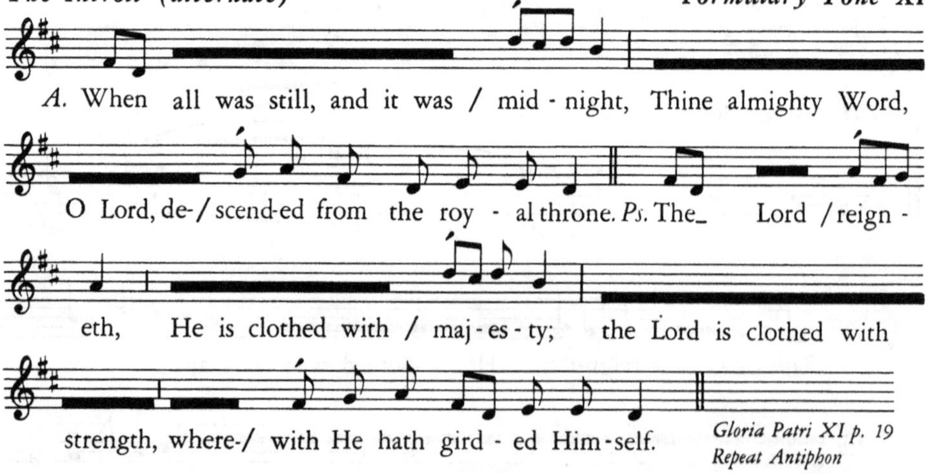
A. When all was still, and it was / mid - night, Thine almighty Word,
O Lord, de-/ scend-ed from the roy - al throne. Ps. The_ Lord / reign -
eth, He is clothed with / maj - es - ty; the Lord is clothed with
strength, where-/ with He hath gird - ed Him - self.
Gloria Patri XI p. 19
Repeat Antiphon

The Circumcision and the Name of Jesus

The Introit *Formulary Tone XI*

A. O— Lord, / our Lord, how excellent is Thy name in / all the earth, who hast set Thy / glo-ry a-bove the heav-ens! What is man that Thou art / mindful of him, and the Son of / Man that Thou vis-it-est Him? *Ps.* Thou, O Lord, art our Father and our Re-/deem-er, Thy / name is from ev-er-last - ing.

Gloria Patri XI p. 19
Repeat Antiphon

The Introit (alternate) *Formulary Tone XI*

A. At the name of Jesus every / knee should bow of things in heaven and things in / earth and things un-der the earth, and every tongue should confess that Jesus / Christ is Lord, to the / glo-ry of God the Fa-ther. *Ps.* O— Lord, / our Lord, how excellent / is Thy name in all the earth!

Gloria Patri XI p. 19
Repeat Antiphon

The Intervenient Chants 17 *Formulary Tone XII*

The Gradual

R. All the ends of the earth have seen the sal-/ va-tion of our God; make a joyful noise un-/ to the Lord, all the earth. V. The Lord hath made / known His sal-va-tion; His righteousness hath He openly showed in the / sight of the hea-then.

The Alleluia

I-II. Alleluia! Alleluia! Alleluia!

V. God, who at sundry times and in divers / man-ners spake in time / past by the proph-ets, hath in these last days spoken unto / us by His Son.

II. Alleluia!

The Second Sunday After Christmas

The Introit *Formulary Tone XI*

(*The Introit, or its alternate, is the same as for the Sunday after Christmas, p. 14*)

The Intervenient Chants *Formulary Tone XII*

XI

The Gloria Patri for the Christmas Cycle Introits

The Epiphany of Our Lord

The Introit [1]   *Formulary Tone VIII*

A.[2] Behold, the Lord, the / Ruler, hath come, and the kingdom and the power and the glory are / in His hand. Ps.[3] Give the King Thy / judgments, O God, and Thy righteousness / unto the King's Son. G.[4] Glory be to the / Father and to the Son and / to the Holy Ghost; as it was in the be-/ginning, is now, and / ever shall be, world with-/out end. A - men. A.[2] Behold, the Lord, the / Ruler, hath come, and the kingdom and the power and the glory are / in His hand.

1. The complete form of the Introit is presented here as a model for the Epiphany season. 2. Antiphon. 3. Psalmellus. 4. Gloria Patri.

The Intervenient Chants   *Formulary Tone VII*

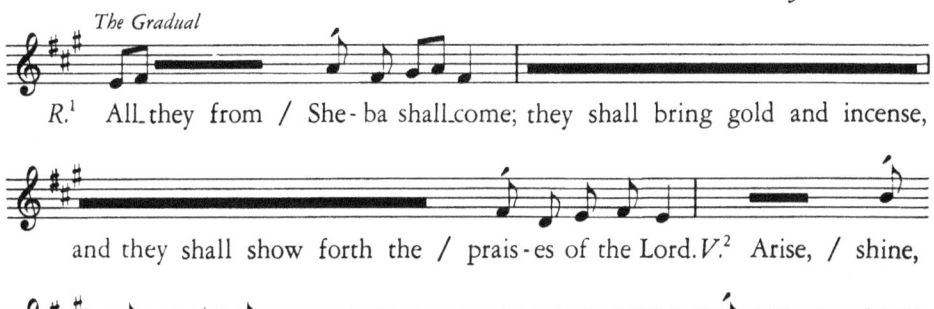

R.[1] All they from / She-ba shall come; they shall bring gold and incense, and they shall show forth the / prais-es of the Lord. V.[2] Arise, / shine, O Je-ru-sa-lem, for the glory of the Lord is / ris-en up-on thee.

I-II.[4] Al-le-lu - - ia! Al - le-lu - - ia!

V.[2] We have seen His / star in the East and are come with gifts to / wor - ship the Lord.

II.[4] Al - le-lu - - ia!

1. Responsorium. 2. Versus. 3. The Alleluia is to be sung immediately upon the conclusion of the Gradual. 4. The jubilant Alleluias should, if at all possible, be sung in four parts (SATB); if not, the upper part may be sung in unison by the whole choir, or by an antiphonal junior or children's choir.

The First Sunday After the Epiphany

The Introit — Formulary Tone VIII

A. I saw also the Lord sitting up-/ on a throne, high and lift-ed up. And I heard the voice of a great / mul-ti-tude, saying: / Al-le-lu-ia! For the Lord God Om-/ nip-o-tent reign-eth. *Ps.* Make a joyful noise unto the / Lord, all ye lands; serve the / Lord with glad-ness.

Gloria Patri VIII, p. 29
Repeat Antiphon

The Introit (alternate) — Formulary Tone VIII

A. On a throne, / high and lift-ed up, I saw a / Man sit-ting whom the multitude of / an-gels a-dores, singing to-/ geth-er: Behold, His dominion en-/ dur-eth for-ev-er. *Ps.* Make a joyful noise unto the / Lord, all ye lands; serve the / Lord with glad-ness.

Gloria Patri VIII, p. 29
Repeat Antiphon

The Intervenient Chants   *Formulary Tone VII*

The Gradual

R. Bless - ed be the Lord God, the God of / Is - ra - el, who only / do-eth won-drous things, and bless-ed be His glorious / name for-ev - er. V. The mountains shall bring / peace to Thy peo-ple, and the / hills right-eous-ness.

The Alleluia

I-II. Al - le - lu - - ia! Al - le - lu - - ia!

V. Make a joyful noise unto the / Lord, all ye lands; serve the / Lord with glad - ness.

II. Al - le - lu - - ia!

The Second Sunday After the Epiphany

The Introit   *Formulary Tone VIII*

A. All the earth shall / wor-ship Thee and shall / sing un-to Thee, O God. They shall / sing to Thy name, O / Thou Most High.

Ps. Make a joyful noise unto / God, all ye lands; sing forth the / hon-or of His name, make His / praise glo-rious.

Gloria Patri VIII, p. 29
Repeat Antiphon

The Intervenient Chants   *Formulary Tone VII*

The Gradual

R. The Lord sent His Word and / heal-ed them and delivered them from / their de-struc-tions. V. Oh, that men would praise the / Lord for His good-ness and for His wonderful works to the / chil-dren of men!

The Alleluia

I-II. Alleluia! Alleluia!

V. Praise ye Him, / all His angels; praise ye / Him, all His hosts.

II. Alleluia!

The Third Sunday After the Epiphany

The Introit *Formulary Tone VIII*

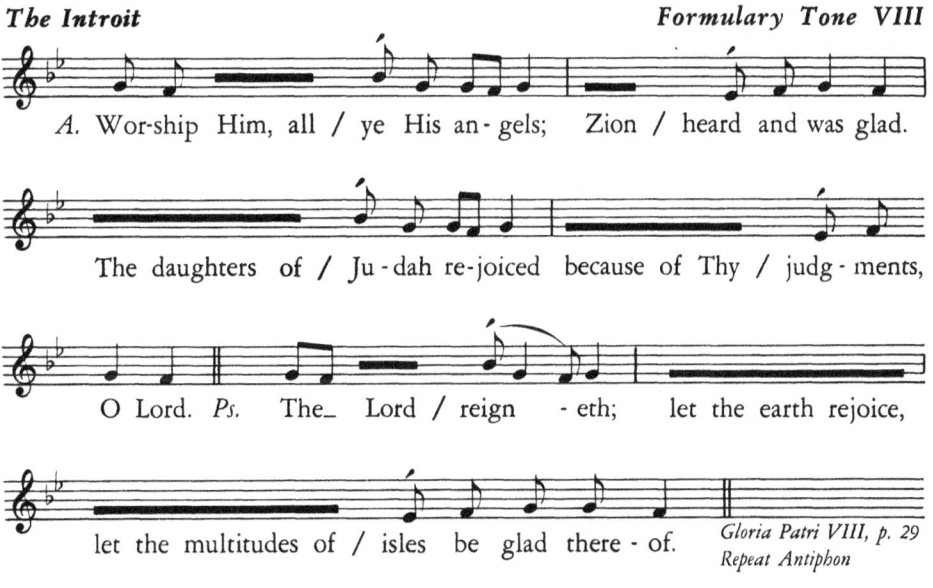

A. Worship Him, all / ye His angels; Zion / heard and was glad.

The daughters of / Judah rejoiced because of Thy / judgments,

O Lord. *Ps.* The Lord / reigneth; let the earth rejoice,

let the multitudes of / isles be glad thereof.

Gloria Patri VIII, p. 29
Repeat Antiphon

26

The Intervenient Chants   *Formulary Tone VII*

The Gradual

R. The heathen shall fear the / name of the Lord, and all the kings of the / earth Thy glory. V. When the Lord shall / build up Zion, He shall ap-/pear in His glory.

The Alleluia

I-II. Al-le-lu-ia! Al-le-lu-ia!

V. The Lord / reign-eth, let the earth rejoice, let the multitude of / isles be glad there-of.

II. Al-le-lu-ia!

The Fourth Sunday After the Epiphany

The Introit   *Formulary Tone VIII*

(The Introit is the same as for the Third Sunday after the Epiphany, p. 25)

The Intervenient Chants   *Formulary Tone VII*

(The Gradual and the Alleluia are the same as for the Third Sunday after the Epiphany, p. 26)

The Fifth Sunday After the Epiphany

The Introit   *Formulary Tone VIII*

(The Introit is the same as for the Third Sunday after the Epiphany, p. 25)

The Intervenient Chants   *Formulary Tone VII*

(The Gradual and the Alleluia are the same as for the Third Sunday after the Epiphany, p. 26)

The Sixth Sunday After the Epiphany (Transfiguration)

The Introit [1]   *Formulary Tone VIII*

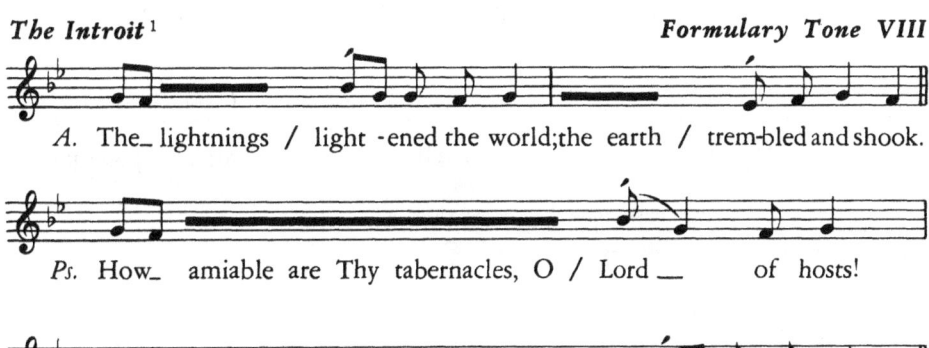

A. The lightnings / light-ened the world; the earth / trem-bled and shook.

Ps. How amiable are Thy tabernacles, O / Lord of hosts!

My soul longeth, yea, even fainteth for the / courts of the Lord.

Gloria Patri VIII, p. 29
Repeat Antiphon

---

1. This Introit, the one for the Transfiguration of our Lord, shall be used on the last Sunday after the Epiphany in each year, except when there is only one Sunday after the Epiphany.

The Intervenient Chants[1]   *Formulary Tone VII*

1. These Intervenient Chants, the ones for the Transfiguration of our Lord, shall be used on the last Sunday after the Epiphany in each year, except when there is only one Sunday after the Epiphany.

VIII

The Gloria Patri for the Epiphany Season Introits

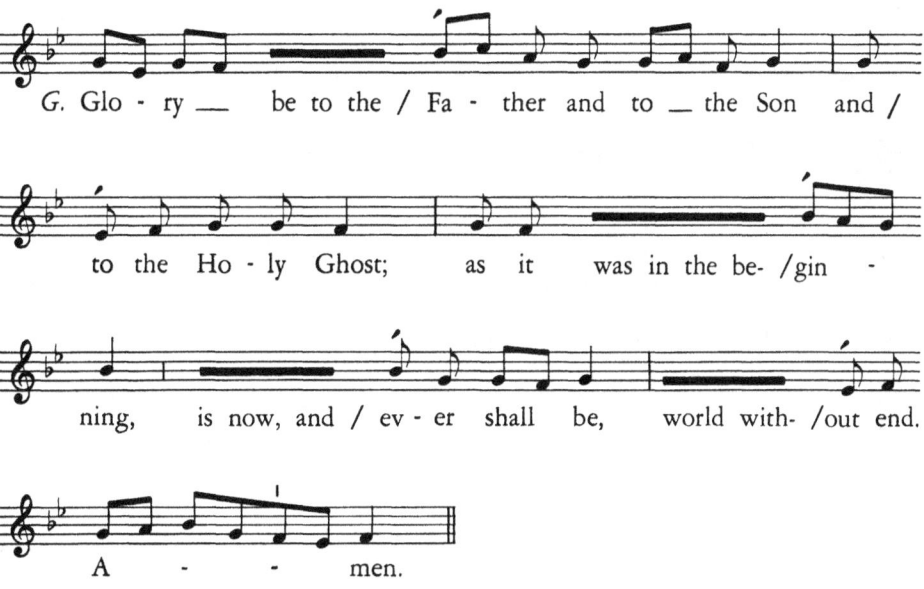

Septuagesima Sunday

The Introit [1] *Formulary Tone IX*

A.[2] The sorrows of death en- / compassed me, the sorrows of hell en- / compassed me about. In my distress I called up-/ on the Lord, and He heard my voice / out of His temple. *Ps.*[3] I will love Thee, O / Lord, my Strength; the Lord is my / Rock and my Fortress. G.[4] Glory be to the / Father and to the Son and / to the Holy Ghost; as it was in the be-/ ginning, is now, and ever / shall be, world with /-out end. A - - - - - men.

A.[2] The sorrows of death en- / compassed me, the sorrows of hell en- / compassed me about. In my distress I called up-/ on the Lord, and He heard my voice / out of His temple.

1. The complete form of the Introit is presented here as a model for the pre-Lent cycle. 2. Antiphon. 3. Psalmellus. 4. Gloria Patri.

The Intervenient Chants   *Formulary Tone* X

1. The Gradual and the Tract may be sung consecutively by one choir; or, the Gradual may be sung by one group (e.g., senior choir) and the Tract by another (e.g., junior choir, children's choir, or few-voiced ensemble). 2. Responsorium. 3. Versus. 4. Tract.

Sexagesima Sunday

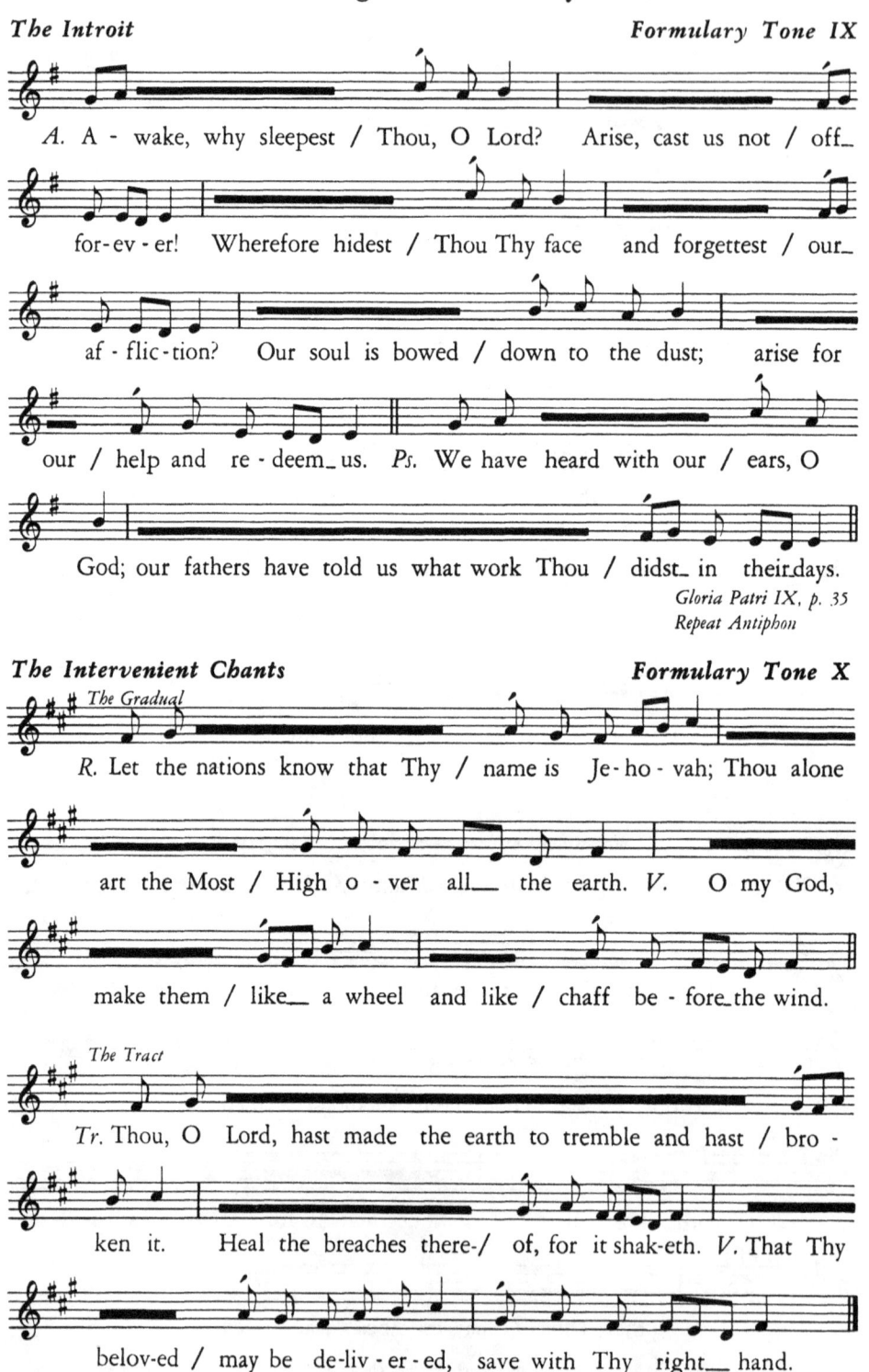

Quinquagesimo Sunday

33

The Introit — *Formulary Tone IX*

A. Be— Thou my / strong— Rock, for an house of de-/ fense— to save me. Thou art my Rock and my / For-tress; therefore for Thy name's sake / lead me and guide me. *Ps.* In— Thee, O Lord, do I / put my trust; let me never be ashamed; deliver me / in— Thy right-eous-ness.

Gloria Patri IX, p. 35
Repeat Antiphon

The Intervenient Chants — *Formulary Tone X*

The Gradual

R. Thou art the God that / do-est won-ders; Thou hast declared Thy strength a-/ mong the peo-ples. *V.* Thou hast with Thine arm re-/ deemed Thy peo-ple, the sons of / Ja-cob and Jo-seph.

The Tract

Tr. Make a joyful noise unto the / Lord—, all ye lands; serve the Lord with gladness. Enter into His / gates with thanks-giv-ing. *V.* Know ye that the / Lord, He is God. It is He that hath made us, and / not— we our-selves; we are His people and the / sheep of His pas-ture.

IX

The Gloria Patri for the pre-Lent Season Introits

Ash Wednesday, the First Day of Lent

The Introit[1]   *Formulary Tone IV*

A.[2] I will / cry un-to God most High, unto God that per-/ form-eth all things for me. Yea, in the shadow of Thy wings will I / make my ref-uge, until these calami- / ties be o-ver-past.

Ps.[3] Be— merciful unto / me—, O God, be / mer-ci-ful un-to me; for my soul / trust-eth in Thee. G.[4] Glo-ry— be to the / Fa-ther and to— the Son and / to the Ho-ly Ghost; as it was in the be-/ gin - ning, is now, and / ev - er shall be, world with-/ out end. A - - - - - men. A.[2] I will / cry un-to God most High, unto God that per-/ form - eth all things for me. Yea, in the shadow of Thy wings will I / make my ref-uge, until these calami- / ties be o-ver past.

1. The complete form of the Introit is presented here as a model for the Lent season. 2. Antiphon. 3. Psalmellus. 4. Gloria Patri.

1. The Gradual and the Tract may be sung consecutively by one choir; or, the Gradual may be sung by one group (e.g., senior choir) and the Tract by another (e.g., junior choir, children's choir, or few-voiced ensemble). 2. Responsorium. 3. Versus. 4. Tract.

Invocabit, the First Sunday in Lent

The Introit   *Formulary Tone IV*

A. He shall call upon Me, and / I will answer him; I will deliver / him and honor him. With long life will I / satisfy him and show him / My salvation. Ps. He that dwelleth in the secret / place of the Most High shall abide under the shadow / of the Almighty.

Gloria Patri IV, p. 43
Repeat Antiphon

The Intervenient Chants

The Gradual   *Formulary Tone III*

R. For He shall give His / angels charge over thee to / keep thee in all thy ways. V. They shall / bear thee up in their hands lest thou dash thy / foot against a stone.

The Tract

Tr. He that dwelleth in the secret / place of the Most High shall abide under the shadow / of the Almighty. V. I will / say of the Lord: He is my Refuge and my / Fortress, my God; in / Him will I trust. V. He shall cover thee / with His feathers, · and under His / wings shalt thou trust.

Reminiscere, the Second Sunday in Lent

Oculi, the Third Sunday in Lent

The Introit   *Formulary Tone IV*

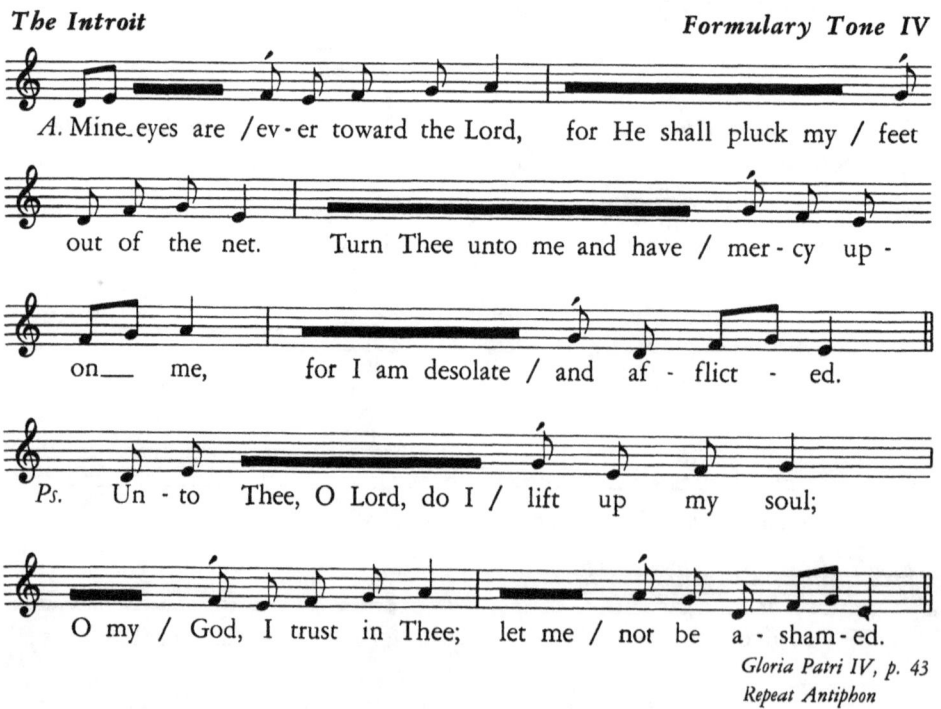

Gloria Patri IV, p. 43
Repeat Antiphon

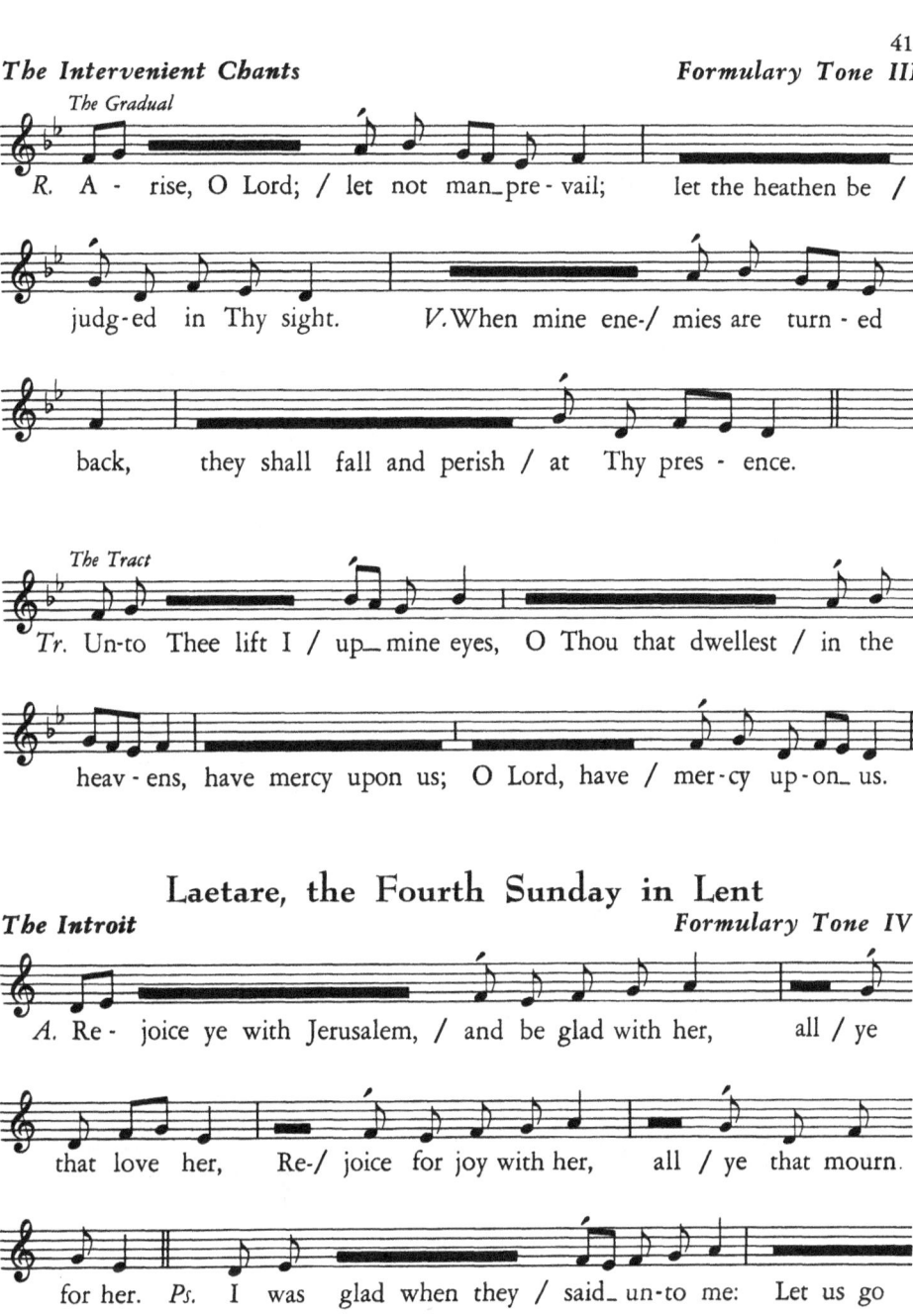

IV

The Gloria Patri for the Lent Season Introits

Judica, the Fifth Sunday in Lent
Passion Sunday

1. The complete form of the Introit is presented here as a model for the Passion season. It is traditional for the Gloria Patri to be omitted during this season. The Antiphon is immediately resumed upon the conclusion of the Psalmellus.
2. Antiphon. 3. Psalmellus.

The Intervenient Chants   *Formulary Tone* IV

The Gradual [1]

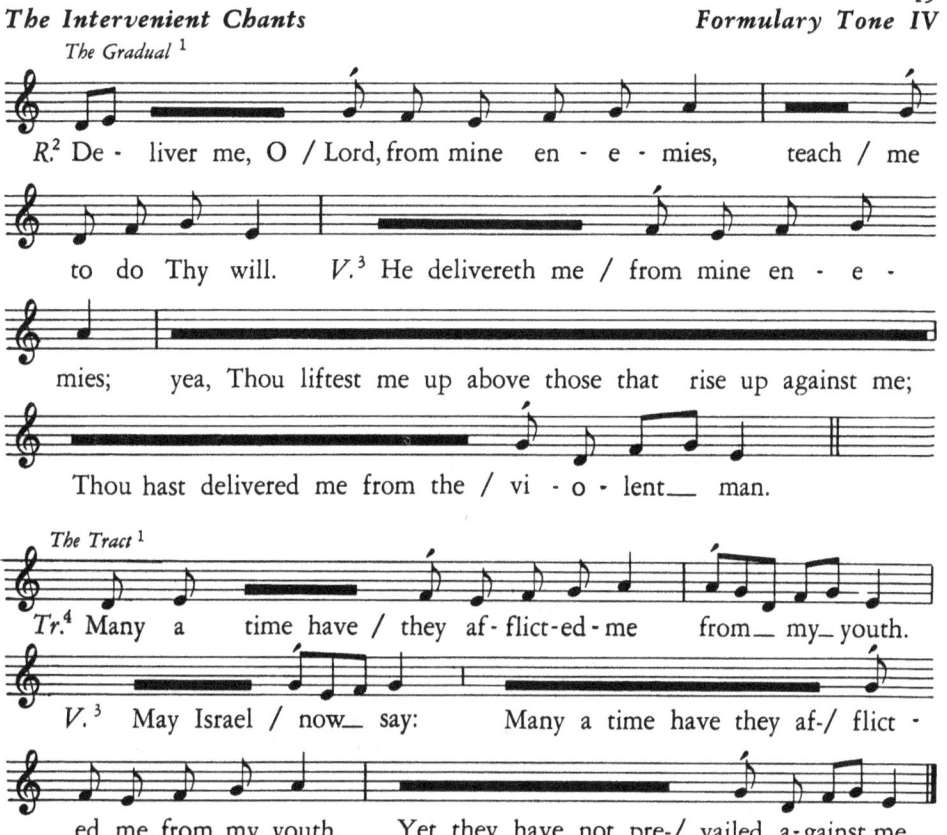

R.[2] De-liver me, O / Lord, from mine en-e-mies, teach / me to do Thy will. V.[3] He delivereth me / from mine en-e-mies; yea, Thou liftest me up above those that rise up against me; Thou hast delivered me from the / vi-o-lent man.

The Tract [1]

Tr.[4] Many a time have / they af-flict-ed-me from my youth. V.[3] May Israel / now say: Many a time have they af-/flict-ed me from my youth. Yet they have not pre-/vailed a-gainst me.

1. The Gradual and the Tract may be sung consecutively by one choir; or, the Gradual may be sung by one group (e.g., senior choir) and the Tract by another (e.g., junior choir, children's choir, or few-voiced ensemble). 2. Responsorium. 3. Versus. 4. Tract.

Palmarum, the Sixth Sunday in Lent

The Introit   *Formulary Tone* III

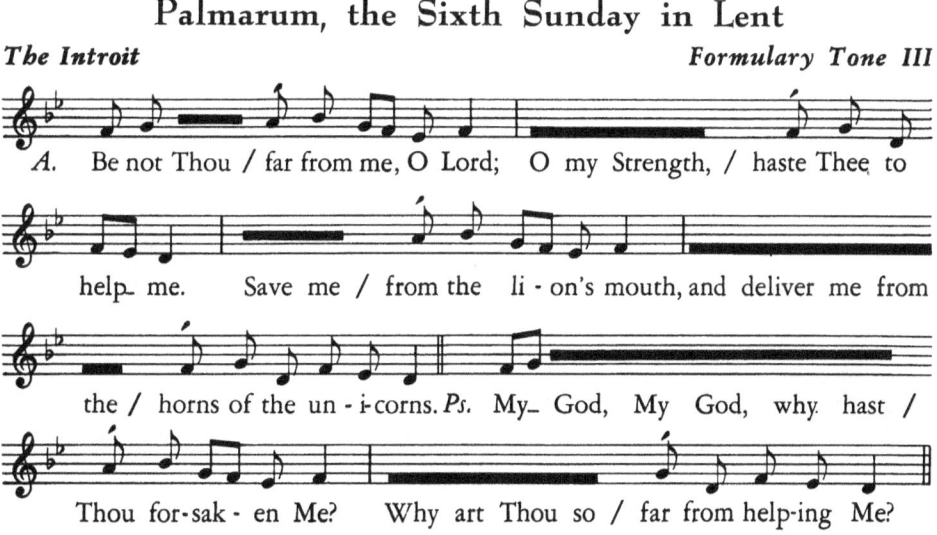

A. Be not Thou / far from me, O Lord; O my Strength, / haste Thee to help me. Save me / from the li-on's mouth, and deliver me from the / horns of the un-i-corns. Ps. My God, My God, why hast / Thou for-sak-en Me? Why art Thou so / far from help-ing Me?

Repeat Antiphon

The Intervenient Chants   *Formulary Tone IV*

The Gradual

R. Thou hast holden me / by my right hand; Thou shalt guide me with Thy counsel and afterward re-/ ceive me to glo - ry.

V. Truly, God is good to Israel, even to such as are of a / clean heart; but as for me, my feet were almost gone, my / steps had well-nigh slipped; for I was griev-ed / at the un - god - ly.

The Tract

Tr. My God, My God, why hast Thou for-/ sak - en Me? Why art Thou so / far from help-ing Me and from the / words of My roar - ing? V. I am a / worm and no man, a reproach of men and de-/ spised of the peo - ple. V. Be not Thou / far from Me, O Lord;

O My Strength, / haste Thee to help Me. *V.* I will declare Thy name un-/ to My brethren; in the midst of the congregation / will I praise Thee. *V.* They shall come and shall declare His righteousness unto a / people that shall be born, that / He hath done this.

Monday of Holy Week

The Introit   *Formulary Tone III*

A. Plead my cause, O Lord, with / them that strive with me; fight against them that / fight a-gainst me. Take hold of / shield and buckler: and / stand up for mine help. *Ps.* Draw out also the spear and stop the way against / them that per-se-cute me; say unto my soul, I am / thy Sal-va-tion. *Repeat Antiphon*

48
The Intervenient Chants   *Formulary Tone IV*

The Gradual

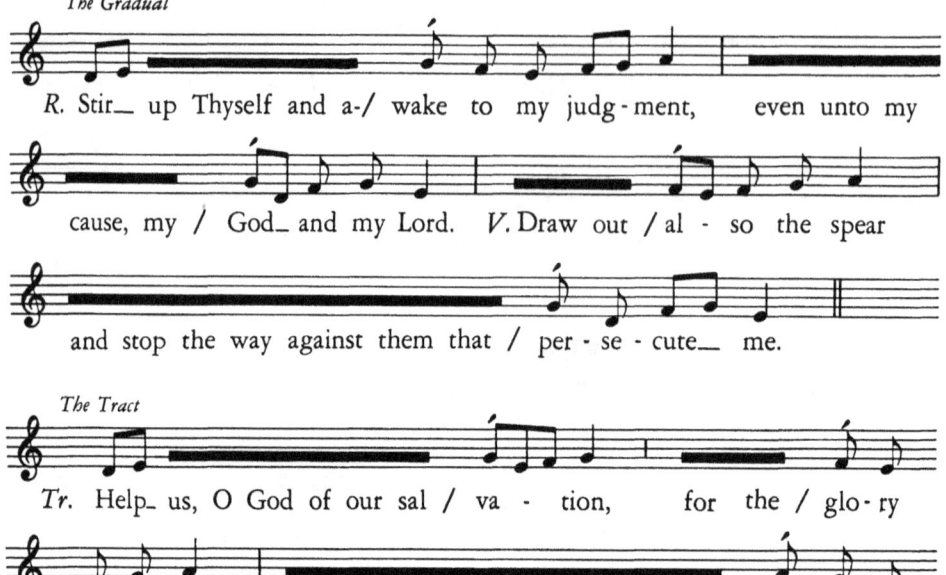

R. Stir up Thyself and a-/ wake to my judg-ment, even unto my cause, my / God and my Lord. V. Draw out / al - so the spear and stop the way against them that / per - se - cute me.

The Tract

Tr. Help us, O God of our sal / va - tion, for the / glo - ry of Thy name, and deliver us, and purge away our / sins for Thy

name's sake.

Tuesday of Holy Week

The Introit   *Formulary Tone III*

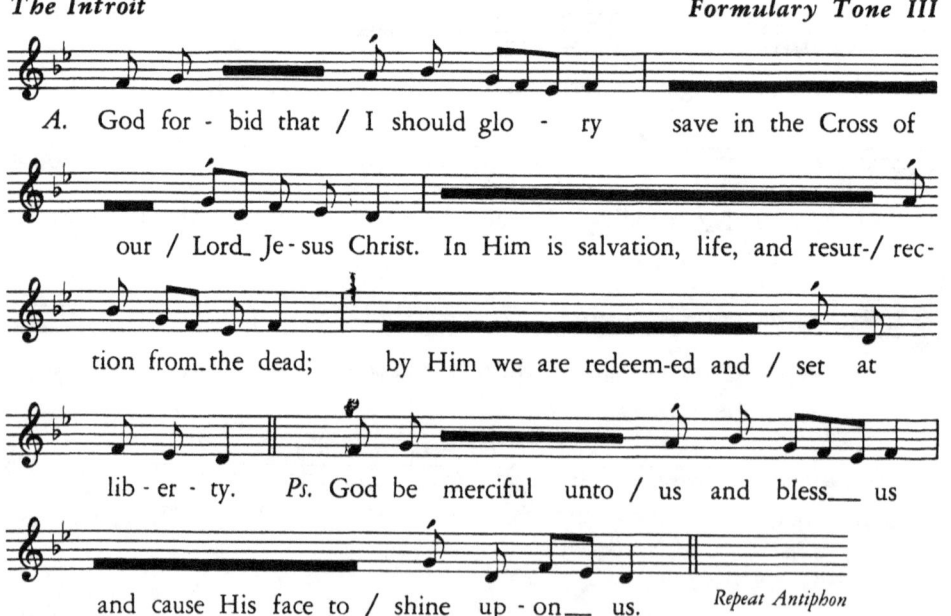

A. God for - bid that / I should glo - ry save in the Cross of our / Lord Je - sus Christ. In Him is salvation, life, and resur-/ rec-tion from the dead; by Him we are redeem-ed and / set at lib - er - ty. Ps. God be merciful unto / us and bless us and cause His face to / shine up - on us. *Repeat Antiphon*

The Intervenient Chant *Formulary Tone IV*

The Gradual [1]

R. As for me, my / cloth-ing was sack-cloth; I humbled my soul

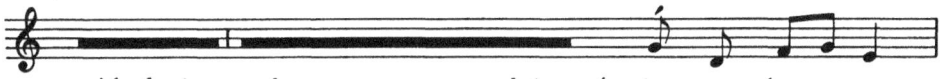
with fasting; and my prayer returned into / mine own bos - om.

V. Plead my cause, O Lord, with / them that strive with me.

Take hold of shield and buckler and / stand up for mine help.

1. The Gradual occurs as a single Intervenient Chant on this day.

Wednesday of Holy Week

The Introit *Formulary Tone III*

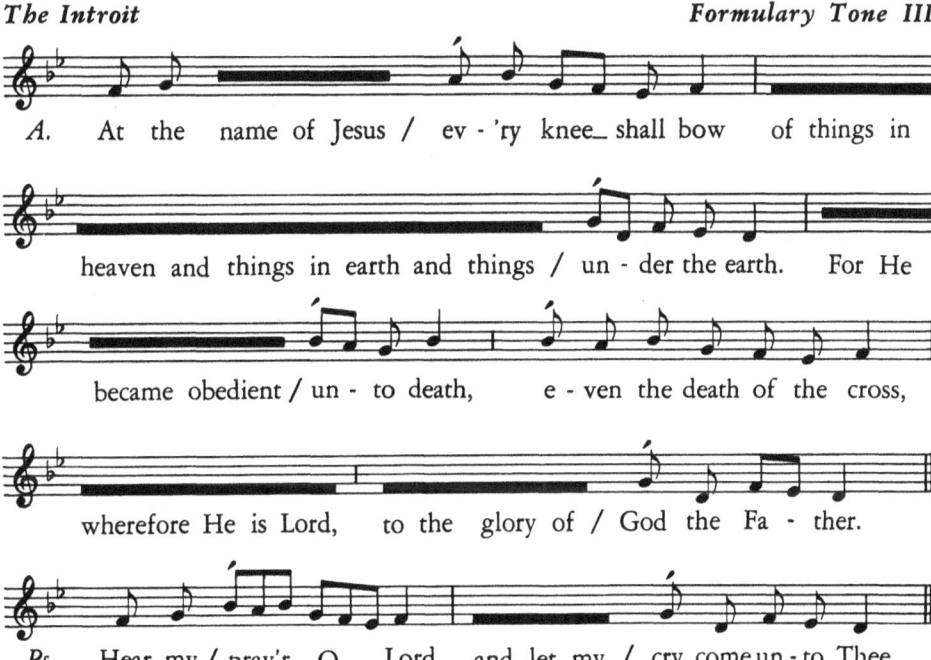
A. At the name of Jesus / ev - 'ry knee shall bow of things in

heaven and things in earth and things / un - der the earth. For He

became obedient / un - to death, e - ven the death of the cross,

wherefore He is Lord, to the glory of / God the Fa - ther.

Ps. Hear my / pray'r, O Lord, and let my / cry come un - to Thee.

Repeat Antiphon

The Intervenient Chants   *Formulary Tone IV*

The Gradual

R. Hide not Thy face from Thy / Serv-ant; for / I am in trou-

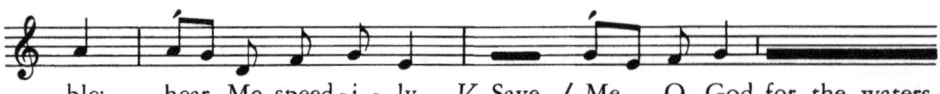
ble; hear Me speed-i-ly. V. Save / Me, O God, for the waters

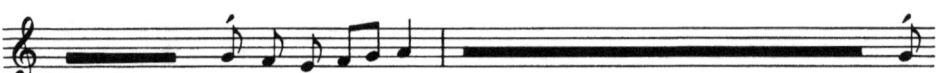
are come / in un-to My soul; I sink in deep mire, where there / is

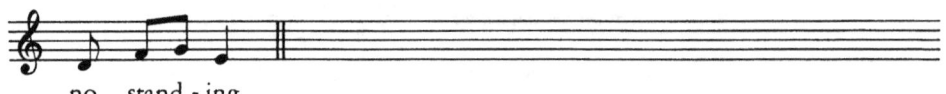
no stand-ing.

The Tract

Tr. Hear my / pray'r, O Lord, and let my / cry come un-to

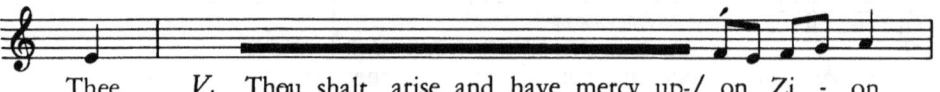
Thee. V. Thou shalt arise and have mercy up-/ on Zi-on,

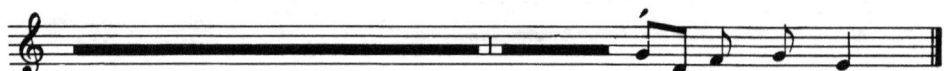
for the time is come to favor her, yea, the / set time is come.

Maundy Thursday

The Introit   **Formulary Tone III**

(The Introit is the same as for Tuesday of Holy Week, p. 48)

The Intervenient Chant   **Formulary Tone IV**

The Gradual [1]

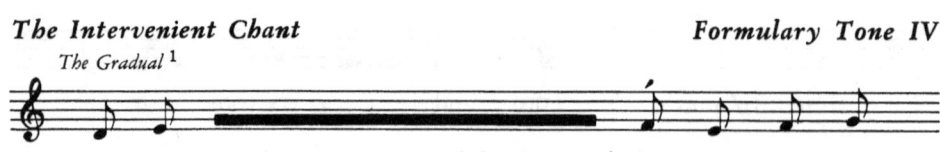
R. Christ hath humbled Himself and become o-/ be-dient un-to

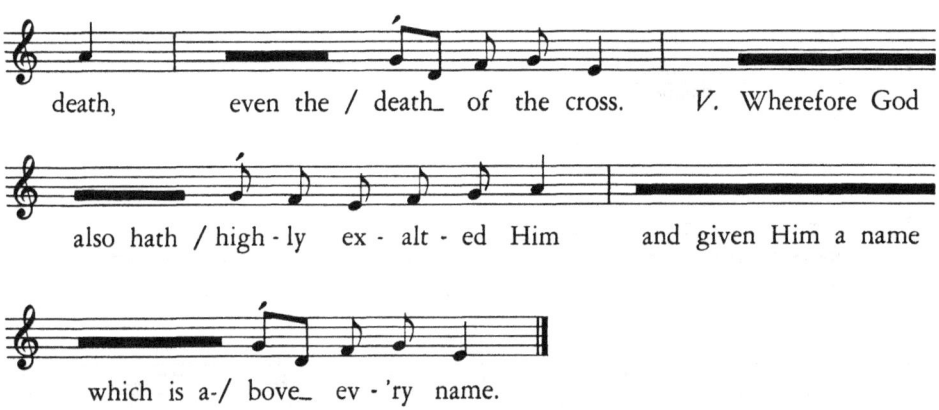

1. Either the Gradual or the succeeding Tract is used as the Intervenient Chant on this day.

The Tract (an alternate chant)   *Formulary Tone IV*

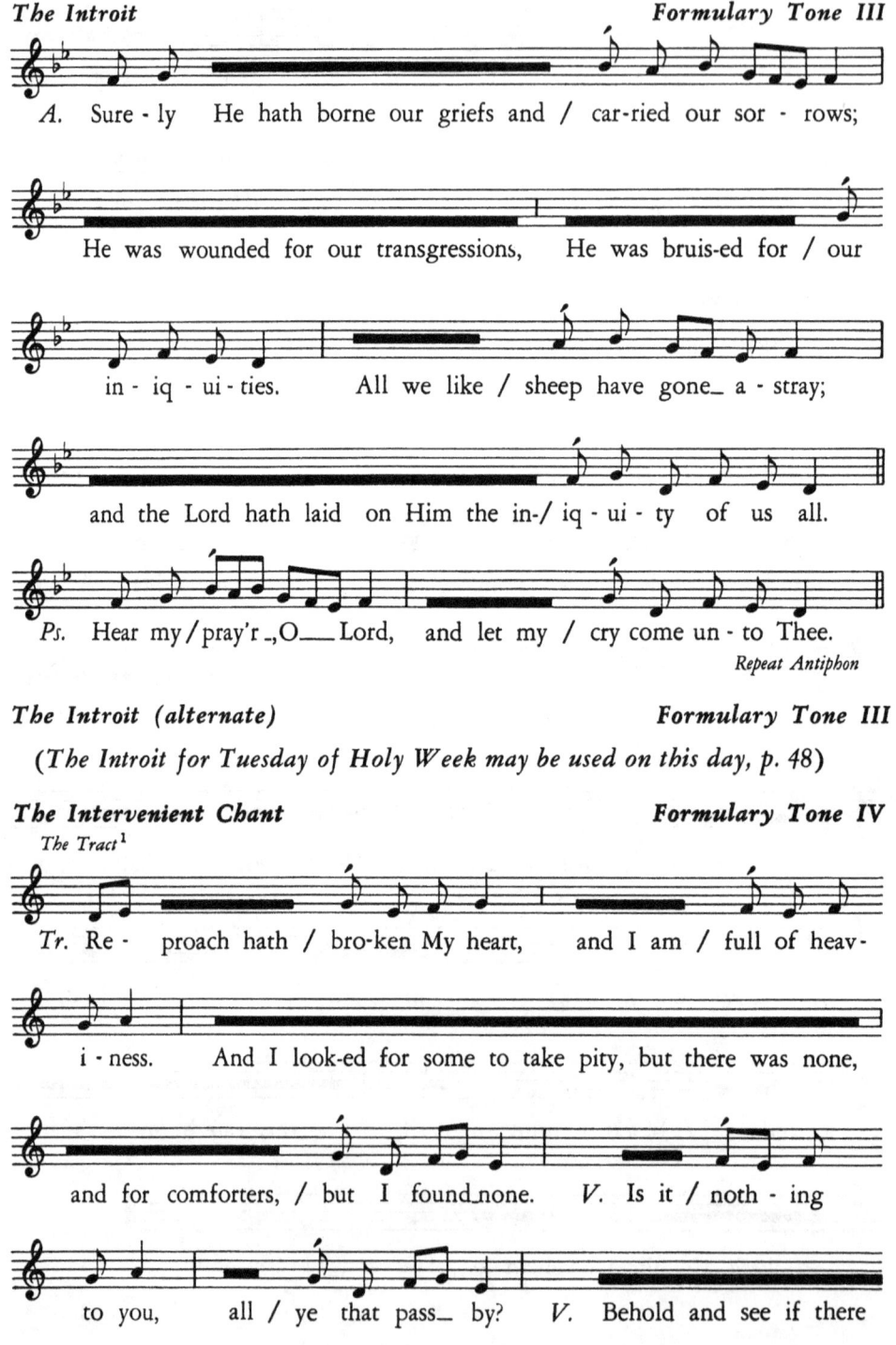

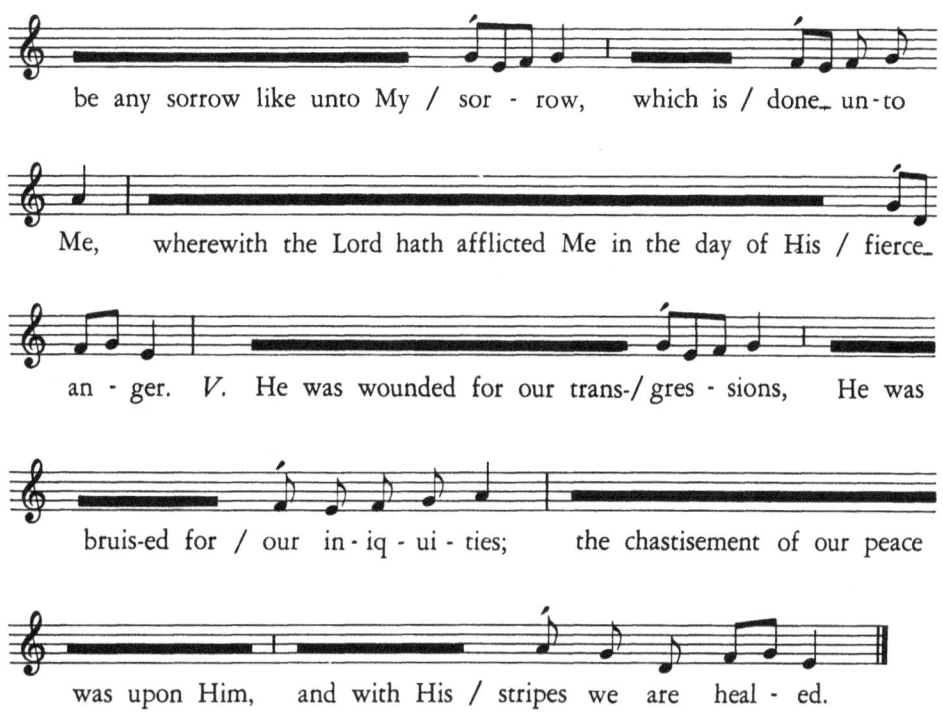

be any sorrow like unto My / sor - row, which is / done un-to Me, wherewith the Lord hath afflicted Me in the day of His / fierce an - ger. *V.* He was wounded for our trans-/gres - sions, He was bruis-ed for / our in - iq - ui - ties; the chastisement of our peace was upon Him, and with His / stripes we are heal - ed.

1. The Tract occurs as a single Intervenient Chant on this day.

Holy Saturday - Easter Eve

The Introit   *Formulary Tone III*

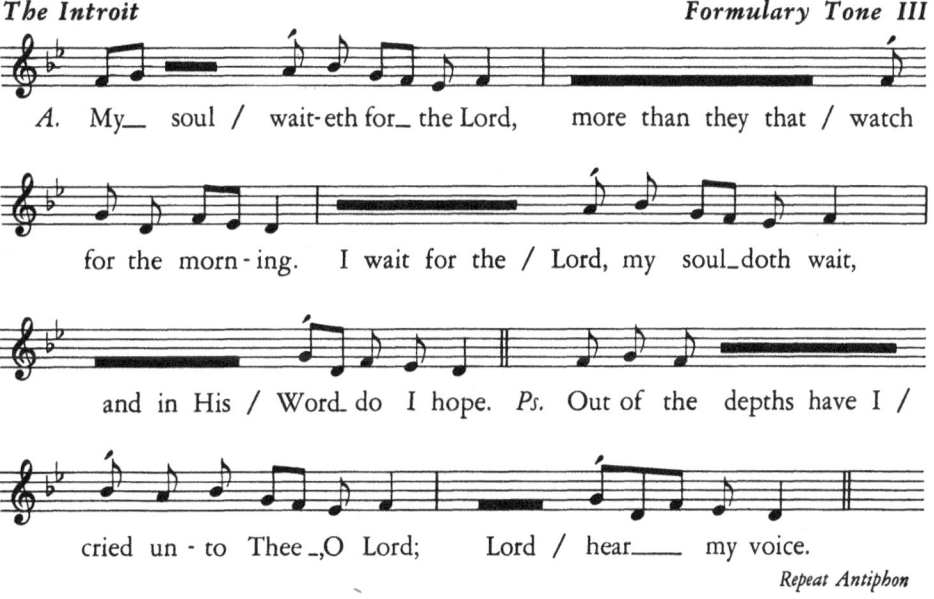

A. My soul / wait-eth for the Lord, more than they that / watch for the morn-ing. I wait for the / Lord, my soul doth wait, and in His / Word do I hope. *Ps.* Out of the depths have I / cried un - to Thee, O Lord; Lord / hear my voice.

Repeat Antiphon

The Intervenient Chant　　　　　　　　　　　　　　　　　　*Formulary Tone IV*

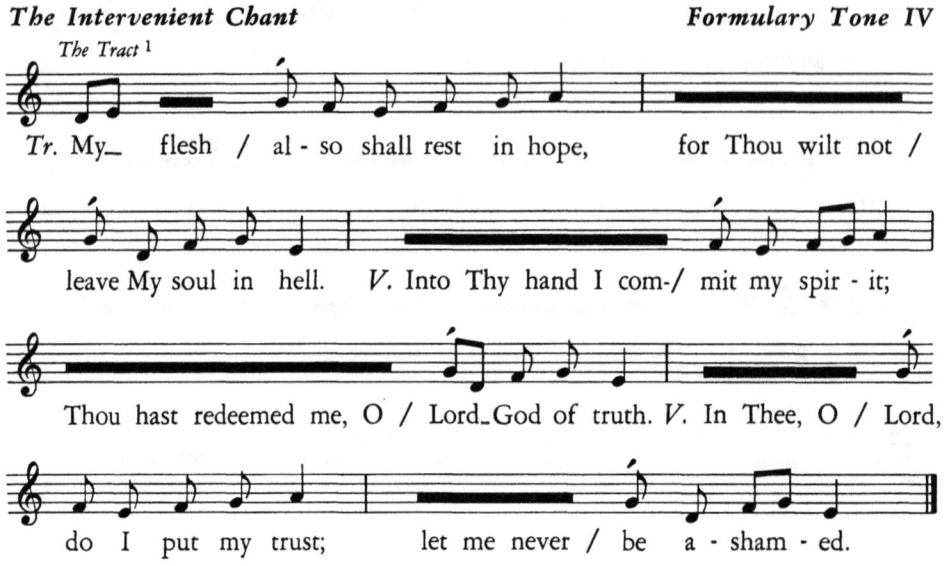

1. The Tract occurs as a single Intervenient Chant on this day.

Easter Day, the Feast of the Resurrection of Our Lord

The Introit[1]   *Formulary Tone VII*

A.[2] When I a-wake, / I am still with Thee. Al-le-lu-ia![3]

Thou hast laid Thine / hand up-on me. Al-le-lu-ia![3]

Such knowledge is too / won-der-ful for me; it is high, I cannot at-/tain un-to it. Al-le-lu-ia! Al-le-lu-ia![3]

Ps.[4] O Lord, Thou hast / searched me and known me; Thou knowest my downsitting and / mine up-ris-ing.

G.[5] Glo-ry be to the / Fa-ther and to the Son and/to the Ho-ly Ghost; as it was in the be-/gin-ning, is now, and / ev-er shall be, world with-/out end. A-men.

1. The complete form of the Introit is presented here as a model for the Paschal season. 2. Antiphon. 3. The jubilant Alleluias should be sung in unison by the choir or by an antiphonal choral group. 4. Psalmellus. 5. Gloria Patri.

The Introit (alternate)   *Formulary Tone VII*

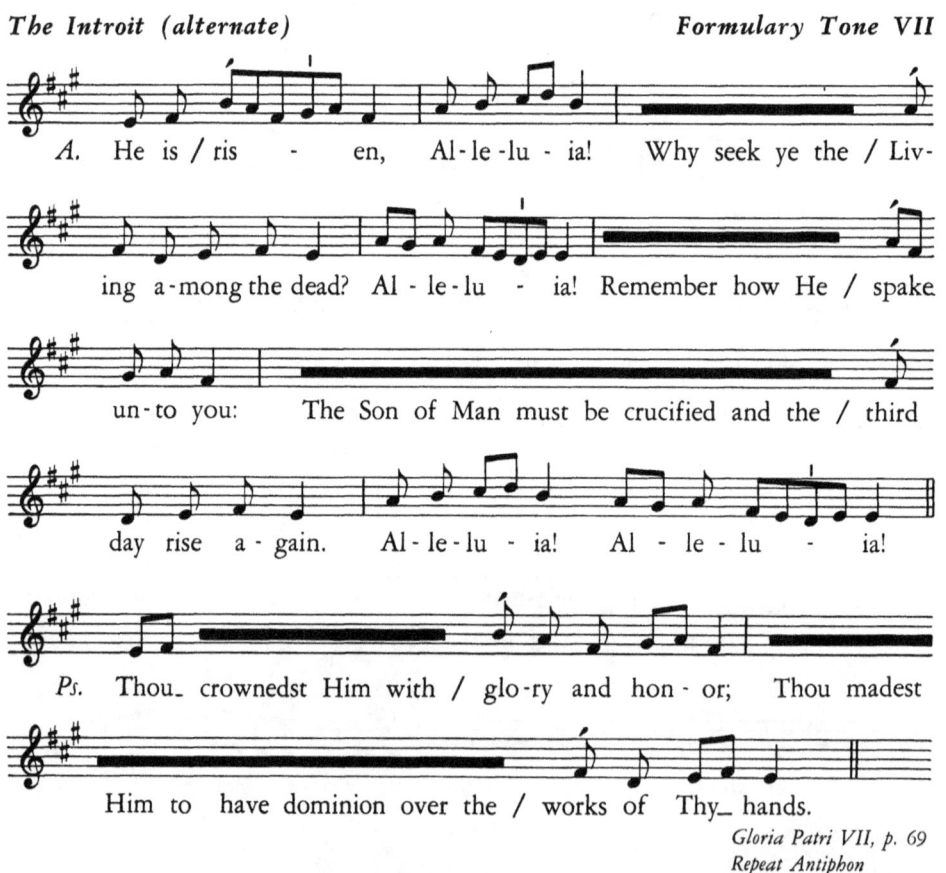

Gloria Patri VII, p. 69
Repeat Antiphon

The Intervenient Chants   **Formulary Tone VIII**

The Gradual

R.[1] This is the day which the / Lord hath made; we will re-/ joice and be glad in it. V.[2] Oh, give thanks unto the / Lord, for He is good, for His mercy en-/ dur-eth for - ev - er.

The Greater Alleluia [3]

I-II.[4] Al - le - lu - - - ia! Al - - le - lu - - - ia!

V.[2] Christ, our / Pass - o - ver, is sacri-/ ficed for us.

II.[4] Al - - le - lu - - ia!

V.[2] Let us / keep the feast with the unleavened bread of sin-/ cer -

1. Responsorium. 2. Versus. 3. The Greater Alleluia is to be sung immediately upon conclusion of the Gradual. 4. The jubilant Alleluias should, if at all possible, be sung in four parts (SATB); if not, the upper part may be sung in unison by the whole choir or by an antiphonal junior or children's choir.

Easter Monday

The Introit   *Formulary Tone VII*

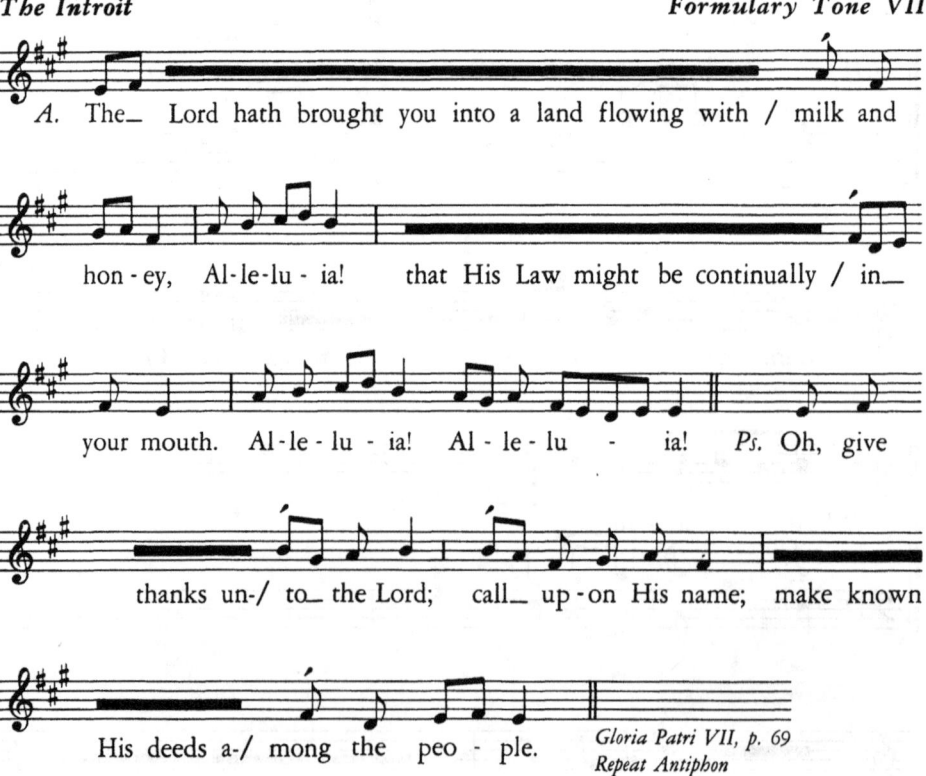

A. The Lord hath brought you into a land flowing with / milk and honey, Al-le-lu-ia! that His Law might be continually / in your mouth. Al-le-lu-ia! Al-le-lu-ia! *Ps.* Oh, give thanks un-/ to the Lord; call upon His name; make known His deeds a-/ mong the peo-ple. *Gloria Patri VII, p. 69*
Repeat Antiphon

The Intervenient Chants *Formulary Tone VIII*

The Gradual

R. This is the day which the / Lord hath made; we will re-/joice and be glad in it. V. Let / Is-ra-el now say, that His mercy en-/dur-eth for-ev-er.

The Alleluia

I-II. Al-le-lu-ia! Al-le-lu-ia!

V. Did not our hearts burn within us while He talked with / us by the way and while He opened to / us the Scrip-tures?

II. Al-le-lu-ia!

Easter Tuesday

The Introit — *Formulary Tone VII*

A. He gave them to drink of the / water of wisdom, Alleluia! and they will be / strengthened thereby, Alleluia! And they shall / not be moved, and it will ex-/ alt them forever. Alleluia! Alleluia!

Ps. Oh, give thanks un-/to the Lord, call upon His name, make known His deeds a-/ mong the people. *Gloria Patri VII, p. 69. Repeat Antiphon*

The Intervenient Chants — *Formulary Tone VIII*

(*The Gradual and the Alleluia are the same as for Easter Monday, p. 59*)

Quasimodogeniti, the First Sunday After Easter

The Introit — *Formulary Tone VII*

A. As / new born babes, Alleluia! desire the sincere / milk

V. The angel of the Lord de-/ scend-ed from heav'n and came

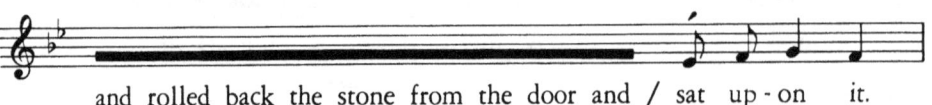

and rolled back the stone from the door and / sat up-on it.

II. Al - le-lu - - ia!

Misericordias Domini, the Second Sunday After Easter

The Introit *Formulary Tone VII*

A. The earth is full of the / good-ness of the Lord, Al-le-lu - ia!

By the word of the / Lord were the heav-ens made. Al-le-lu - ia!

Al - le-lu - ia! *Ps.* Re - joice in the / Lord,

O ye right-eous, for praise is come-ly / for the up-right.

Gloria Patri VII, p. 69
Repeat Antiphon

The Intervenient Chant — Formulary Tone VIII

64

Jubilate, the Third Sunday After Easter

The Introit *Formulary Tone VII*

A. Make a joyful noise unto / God,. all ye lands, Al-le-lu-ia! Sing forth the honor of His name, make His / praise. glo-rious. Al-le-lu-ia! Al-le-lu--ia! Ps. Say un-to God: How terrible / art Thou in Thy works! Through the greatness of Thy power shall Thine enemies submit them-/ selves. un-to Thee. *Gloria Patri VII, p. 69*
Repeat Antiphon

The Intervenient Chant *Formulary Tone VIII*

The Greater Alleluia

I-II. Al-le-lu--ia! Al-le-lu--ia!

V. The_ Lord hath / sent re-demp-tion un-/to His peo-ple.

II. Al - - le - lu - - ia!

V. It behoov-ed Christ to suffer and to / rise__ from the dead and thus to en-ter in-/ to His glo - ry.

II. Al - - le - lu - - - ia!

Cantate, the Fourth Sunday After Easter

The Introit   *Formulary Tone VII*

A. Oh,__ sing unto the / Lord a new__ song, Al - le - lu - ia!

for He hath done / mar - vel - ous__ things. Al - le - lu - - ia!

The Lord hath made / known His sal - va - tion; His righteousness

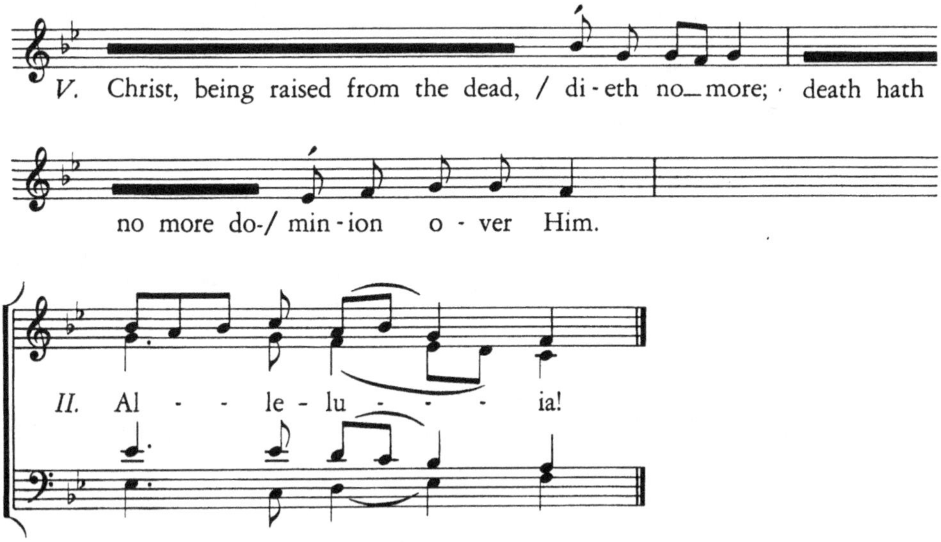

V. Christ, being raised from the dead, / di-eth no more; death hath no more do-/min-ion o-ver Him.

II. Al - le - lu - ia!

Rogate, the Fifth Sunday After Easter

The Introit *Formulary Tone VII*

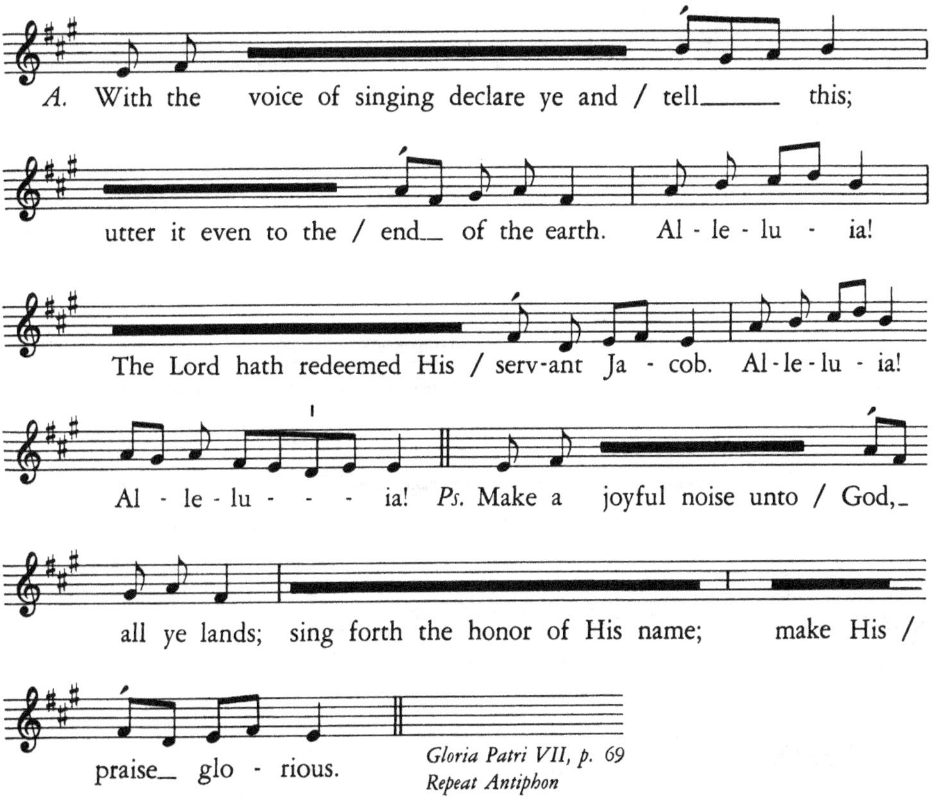

A. With the voice of singing declare ye and / tell this; utter it even to the / end of the earth. Al-le-lu-ia! The Lord hath redeemed His / serv-ant Ja-cob. Al-le-lu-ia! Al-le-lu-ia! *Ps.* Make a joyful noise unto / God, all ye lands; sing forth the honor of His name; make His / praise glo-rious.

Gloria Patri VII, p. 69
Repeat Antiphon

VII

The Gloria Patri for the Paschal Season Introits

70

The Ascension of Our Lord

71

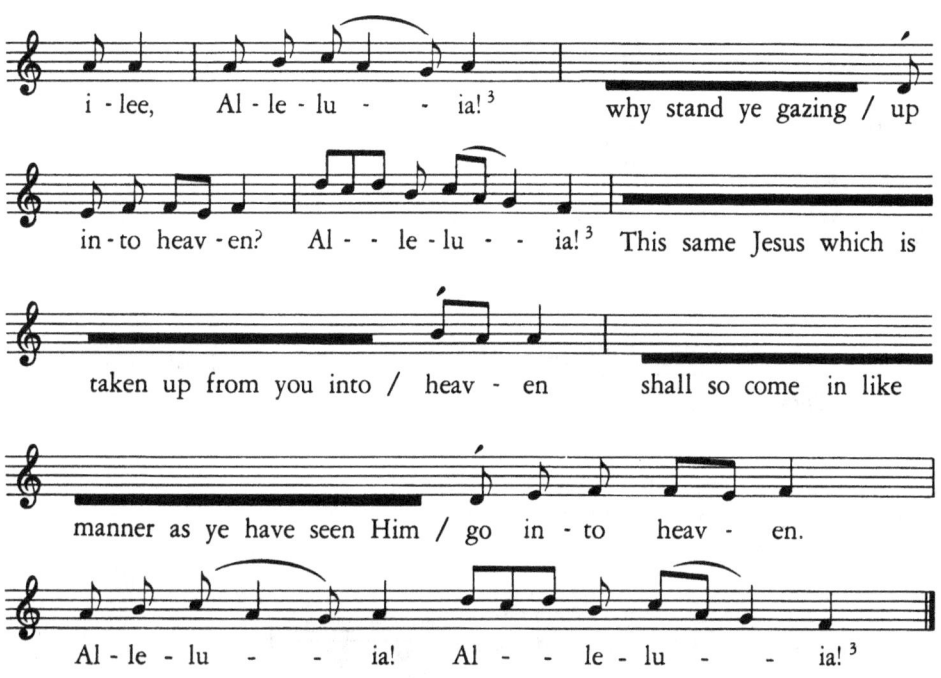

1. The complete form of the Introit is presented here as a model for Ascension and Whitsuntide. 2. Antiphon. 3. The jubilant Alleluias should be sung in unison by the choir or by an antiphonal choral group. 4. Psalmellus. 5. Gloria Patri.

The Intervenient Chant   *Formulary Tone V*

The Greater Alleluia [1]

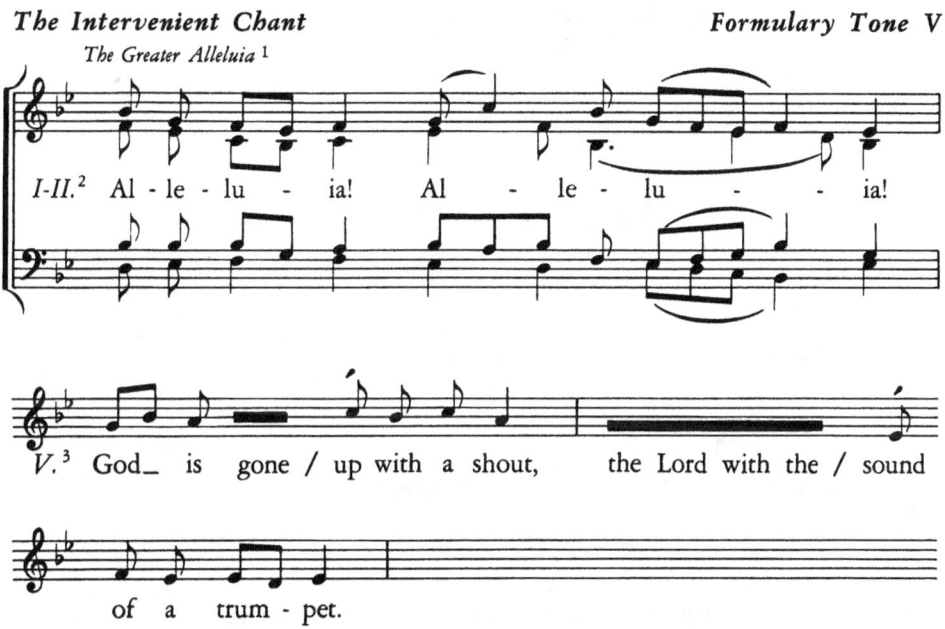

1. The Greater Alleluia serves as a single intervenient chant on this day. 2. The jubilant Alleluias should, if at all possible, be sung in four parts (SATB); if not, the upper part may be sung in unison by the whole choir or by an antiphonal junior or children's choir. 3. Versus.

Exaudi, the Sunday After the Ascension

The Introit   *Formulary Tone VI*

The Intervenient Chant   *Formulary Tone V*

The Greater Alleluia

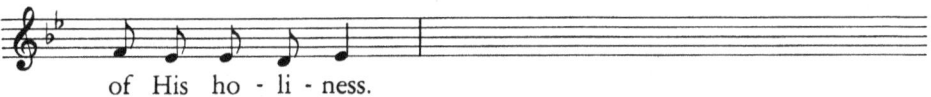

Whitsunday, the Feast of Pentecost

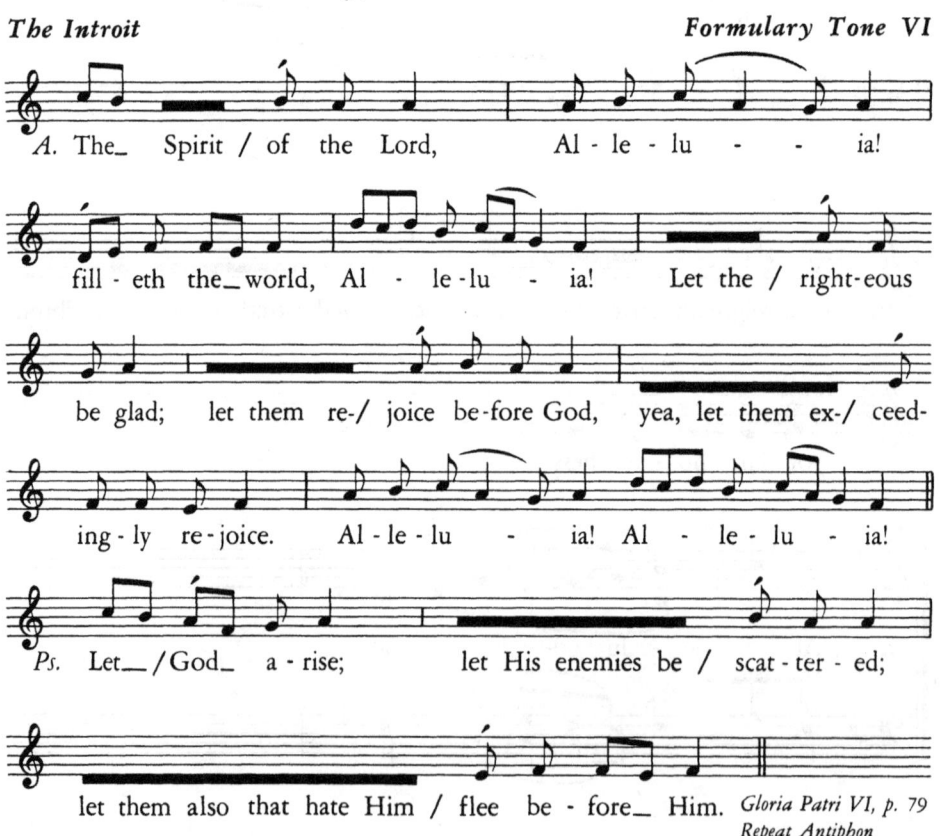

75

The Intervenient Chant *Formulary Tone V*

The Greater Alleluia

Monday of Whitsun-Week

The Introit — Formulary Tone VI

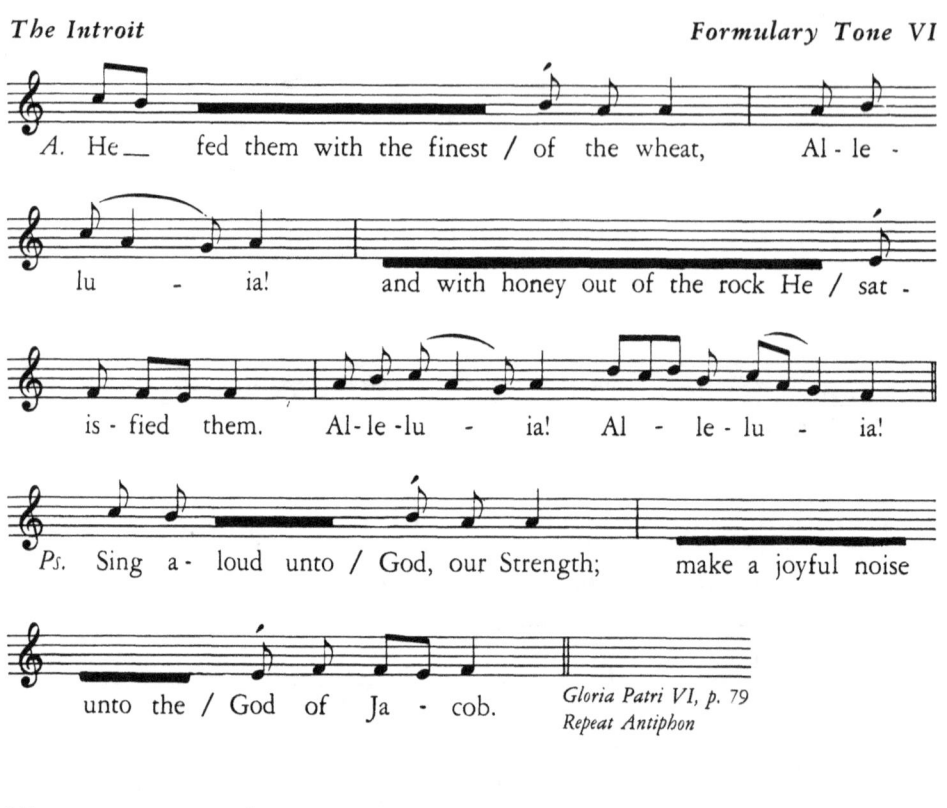

A. He fed them with the finest / of the wheat, Alleluia! and with honey out of the rock He / satisfied them. Alleluia! Alleluia!

Ps. Sing aloud unto / God, our Strength; make a joyful noise unto the / God of Jacob.

Gloria Patri VI, p. 79
Repeat Antiphon

The Intervenient Chant — Formulary Tone V
The Greater Alleluia

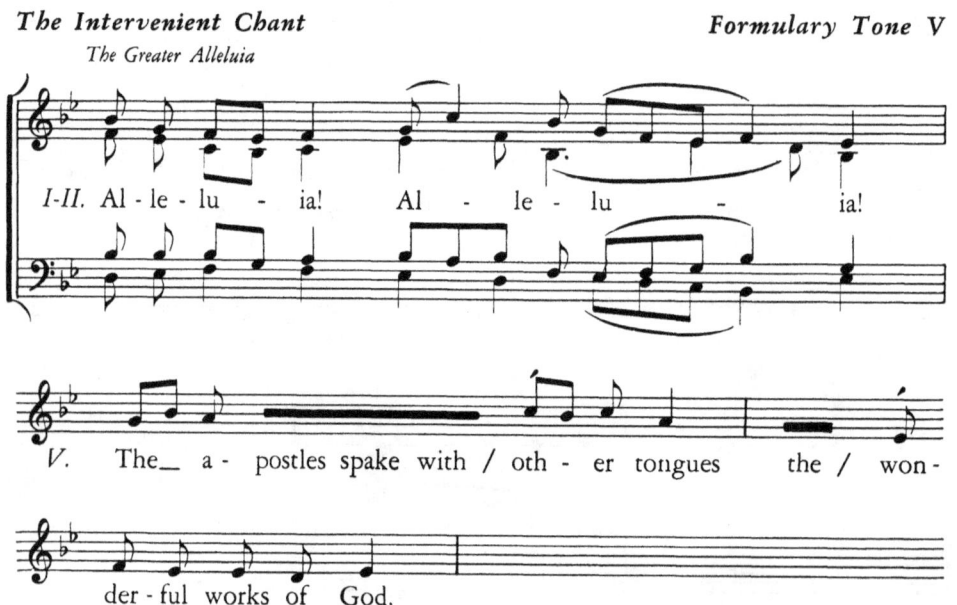

I-II. Alleluia! Alleluia!

V. The apostles spake with / other tongues the / wonderful works of God.

Tuesday of Whitsun-Week

The Introt *Formulary Tone VI*

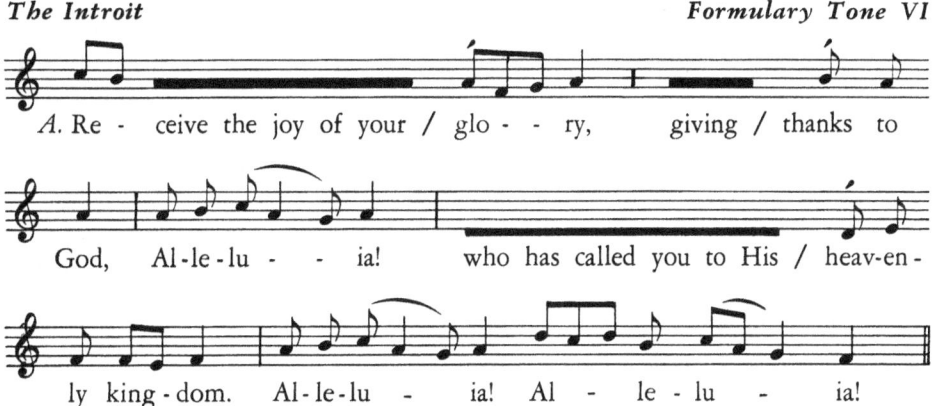

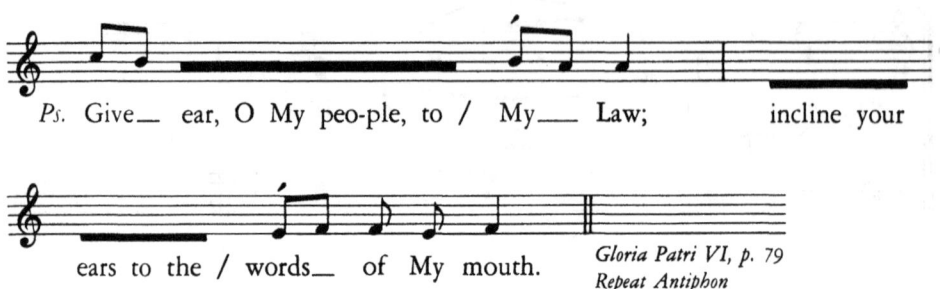

Ps. Give— ear, O My peo-ple, to / My— Law;   incline your ears to the / words— of My mouth.   *Gloria Patri VI, p. 79*
Repeat Antiphon

The Intervenient Chant   ***Formulary Tone V***

(*The Greater Alleluia is the same as for Monday of Whitsun-week, p. 76*)

VI

The Gloria Patri for Ascension and Whitsuntide Introits

The Feast of the Holy Trinity

The Introit[1]   *Formulary Tone XII*

A.[2] Bless-ed be the Holy Trinity and the undi-/ vid-ed U-ni-ty; let us give glory to Him because He hath / shown His mer-cy to us. Ps.[3] O /Lord, our Lord, how excellent / is Thy name in all the earth! G.[4] Glo-ry be to the / Fa-ther and to the Son and /to the Ho-ly Ghost; as it was in the be-/gin-ning, is now, and / ev-er shall be, world with-/out end. A - - - men.

A.[2] Bless-ed be the Holy Trinity and the undi-/ vid-ed U-ni-ty; let us give glory to Him because He hath / shown His mer-cy to us.

---

1. The complete form of the Introit is presented here as a model for the first cycle of the Trinity season. 2. Antiphon. 3. Psalmellus. 4. Gloria Patri.

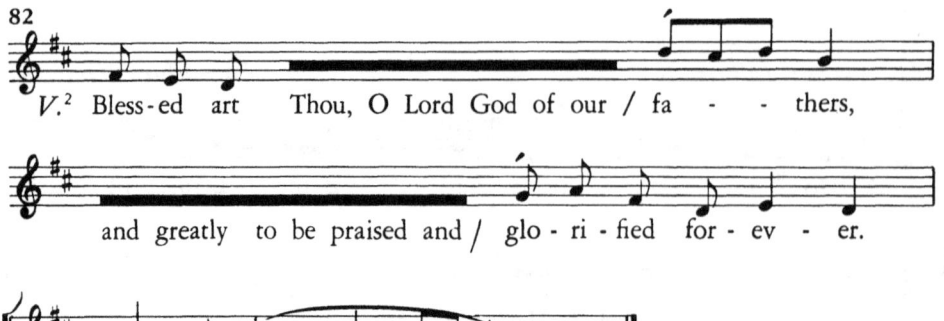

1. Responsorium. 2. Versus. 3. The Alleluia is to be sung immediately upon the conclusion of the Gradual. 4. The jubilant Alleluias should, if at all possible, be sung in four parts (SATB); if not, the upper part may be sung in unison by the whole choir, or by an antiphonal junior or children's choir.

The First Sunday After Trinity

The Introit   *Formulary Tone XII*

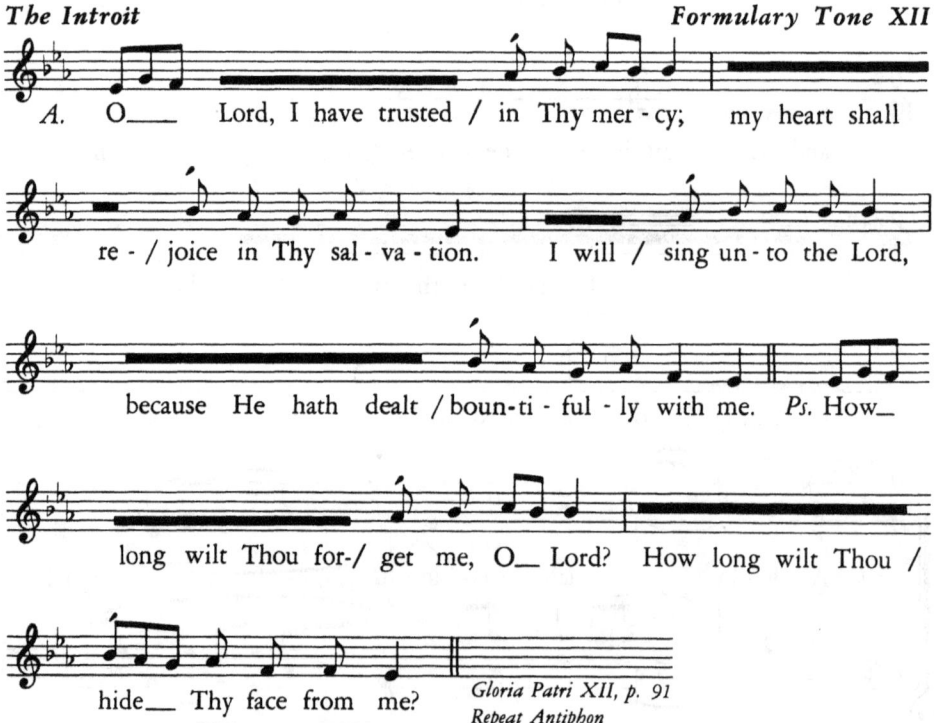

Gloria Patri XII, p. 91
Repeat Antiphon

83

The Intervenient Chants Formulary Tone XI

The Gradual

R. I said, Lord, be merciful / un-to me; heal my soul, for / I have sinned a-gainst Thee. V. Bless-ed is he that con-/ sid-'reth the poor; the Lord will deliver / him in time of trou-ble.

The Alleluia

I-II. Al-le-lu - ia! Al - le-lu - - ia!

V. Give ear to my / words, O Lord; con-/sid-er my med-i-ta-tion.

II. Al - le-lu - - - ia!

The Third Sunday After Trinity

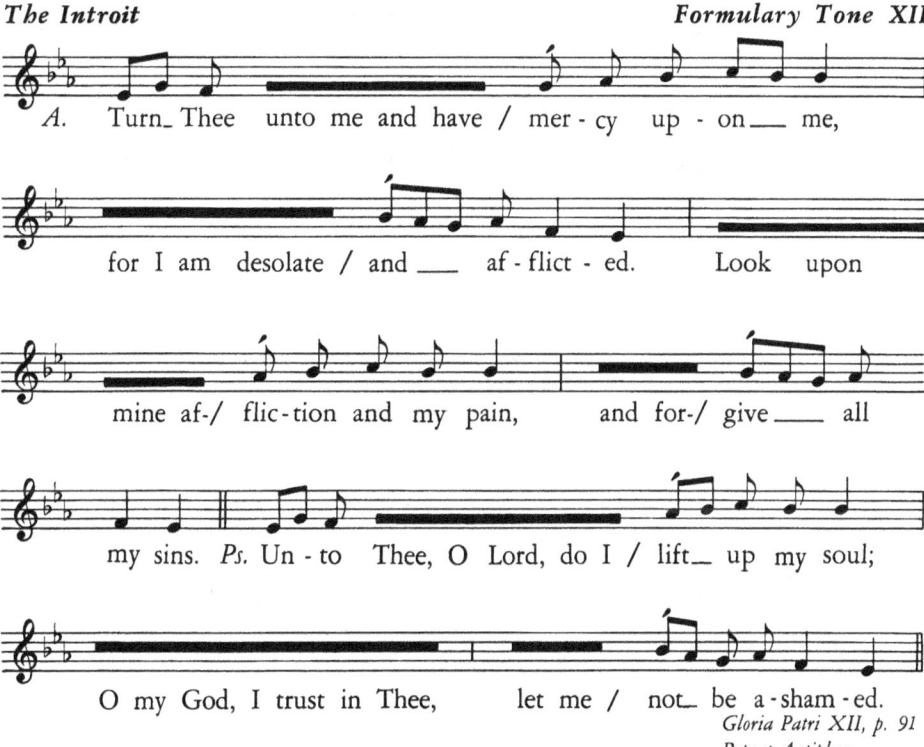

The Fourth Sunday After Trinity

88

The Alleluia

The Fifth Sunday After Trinity

XII

The Gloria Patri for the Introits of the Trinity Season, Cycle I

The Sixth Sunday After Trinity

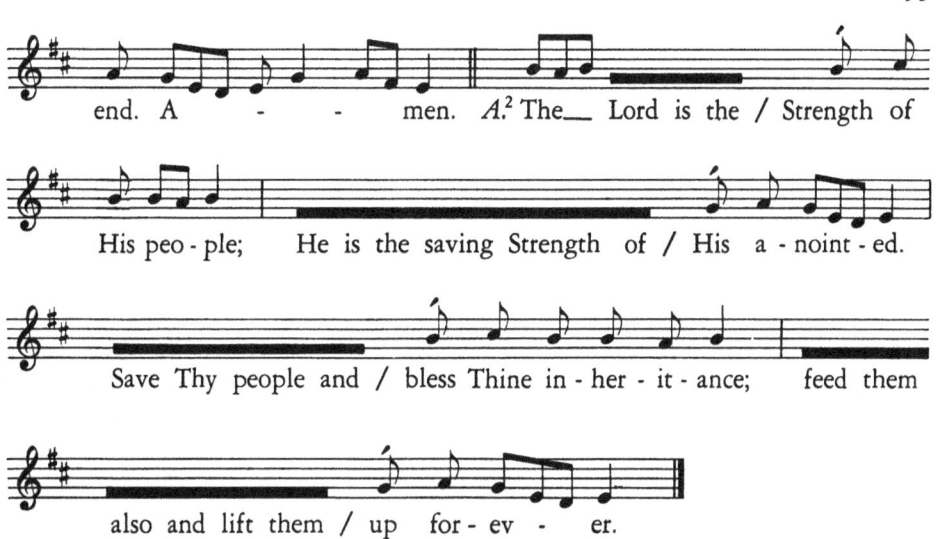

1. The complete form of the Introit is presented here as a model for the second cycle of the Trinity season. 2. Antiphon. 3. Psalmellus. 4. Gloria Patri.

The Intervenient Chants   *Formulary Tone I*

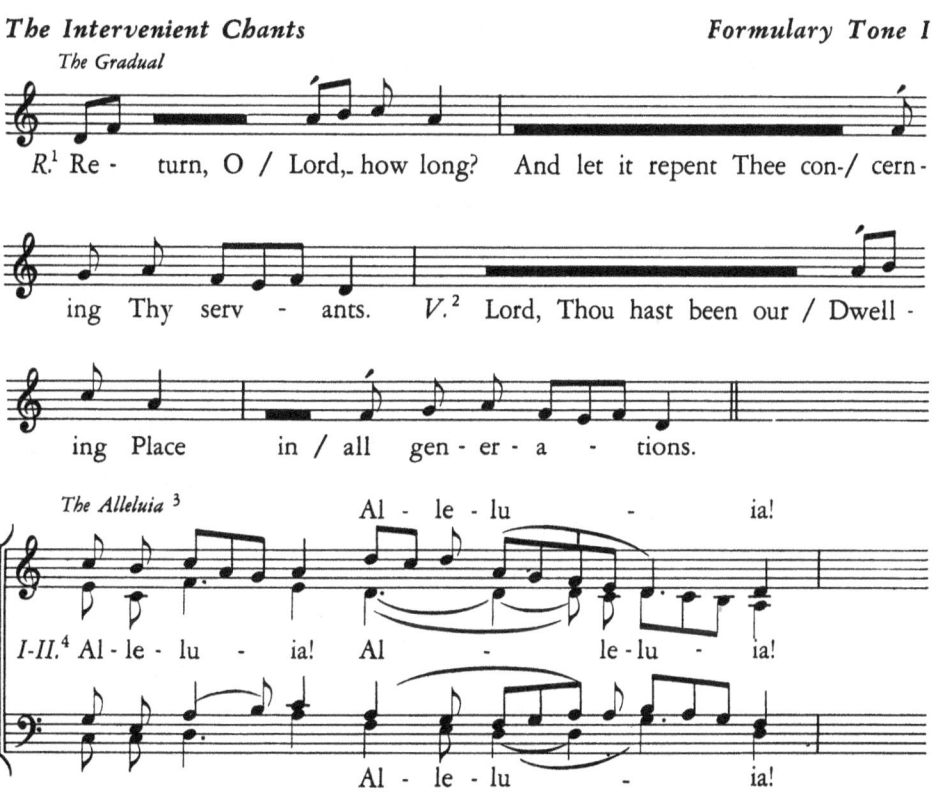

1. Responsorium. 2. Versus. 3. The Alleluia is to be sung immediately upon the conclusion of the Gradual. 4. The jubilant Alleluias should, if at all possible, be sung in four parts (SATB); if not, the upper part may be sung in unison by the whole choir, or by an antiphonal junior or children's choir.

The Seventh Sunday After Trinity

The Introit *Formulary Tone II*

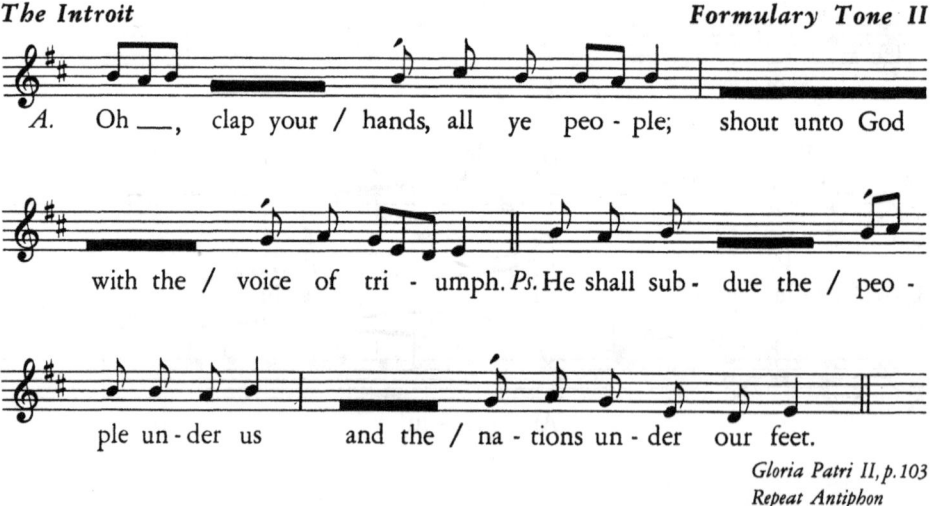

Gloria Patri II, p.103
Repeat Antiphon

The Eighth Sunday After Trinity

The Alleluia

The Ninth Sunday After Trinity

The Introit ***Formulary Tone II***

Gloria Patri H, p. 103

Repeat Antiphon

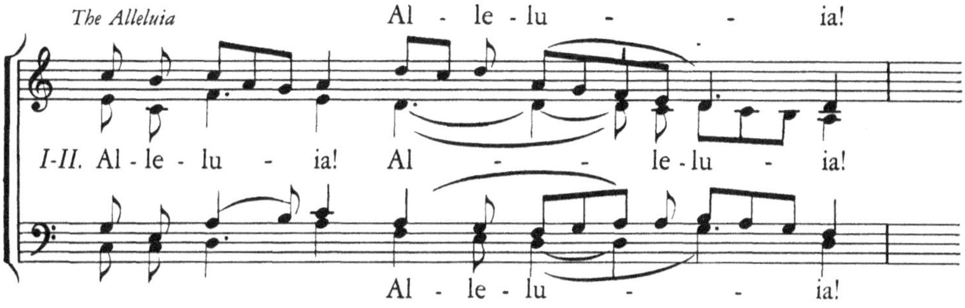

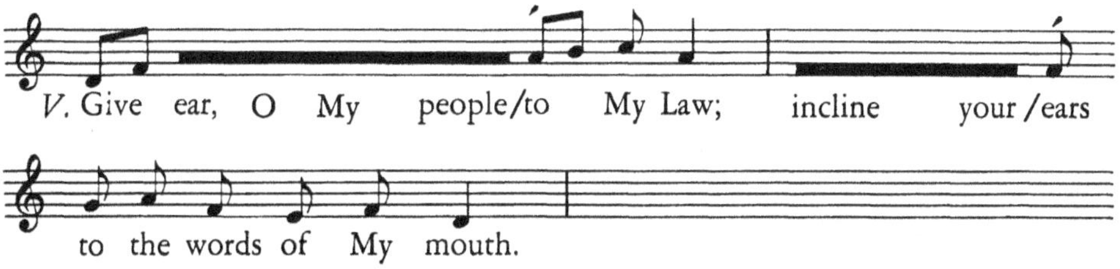

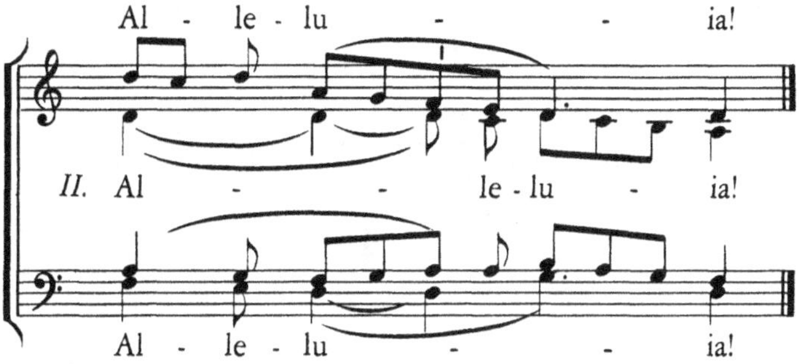

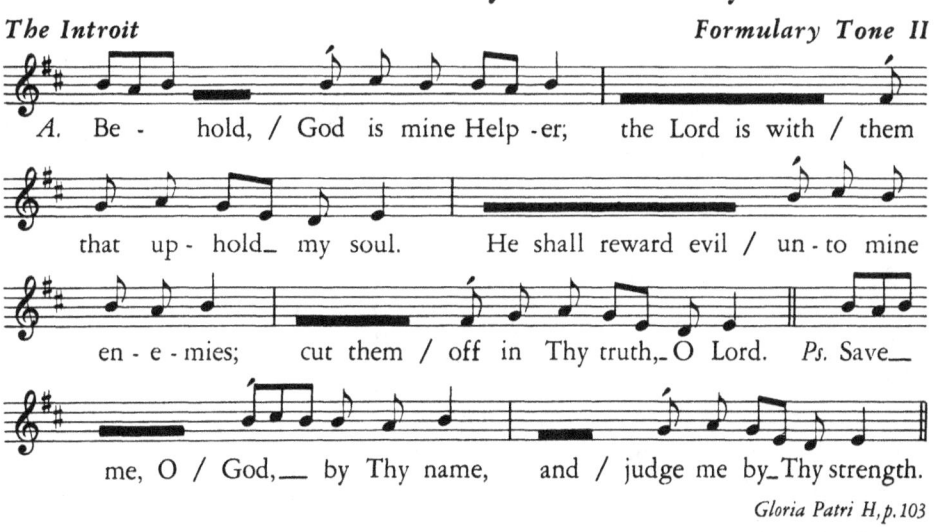

The Intervenient Chants

Formulary Tone I

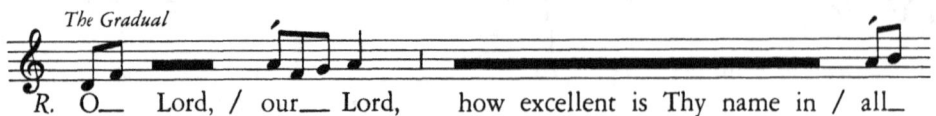
R. O Lord, / our Lord, how excellent is Thy name in / all the earth, who hast set Thy glory a-/ bove the heav-ens!

The Alleluia
I-II. Alleluia! Alleluia! Alleluia!

V. Bless-ed is the man that / fear-eth the Lord, that delighteth greatly / in His com-mand-ments.

II. Alleluia! Alleluia! Alleluia!

The Tenth Sunday After Trinity

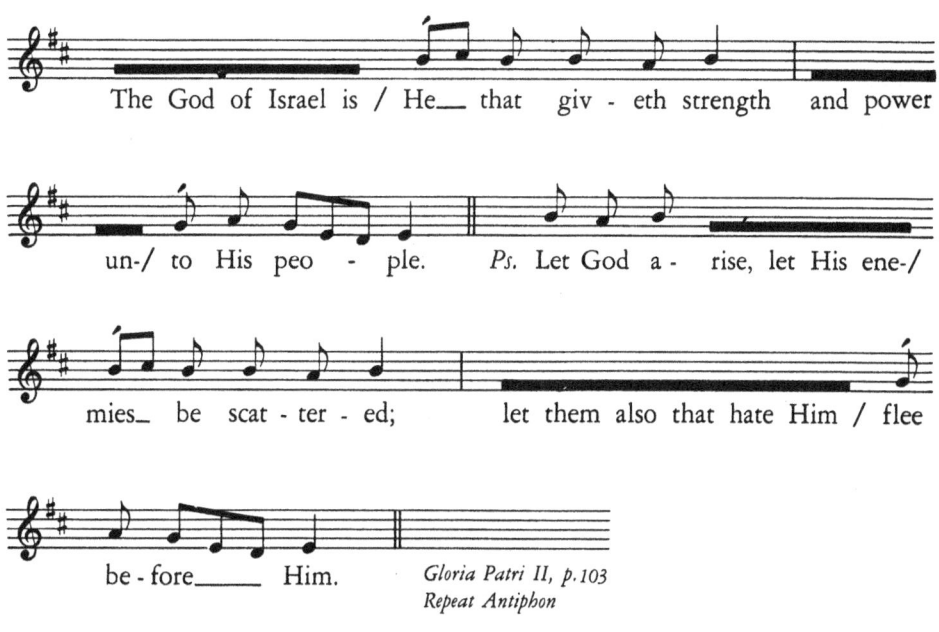

The Intervenient Chants   *Formulary Tone I*

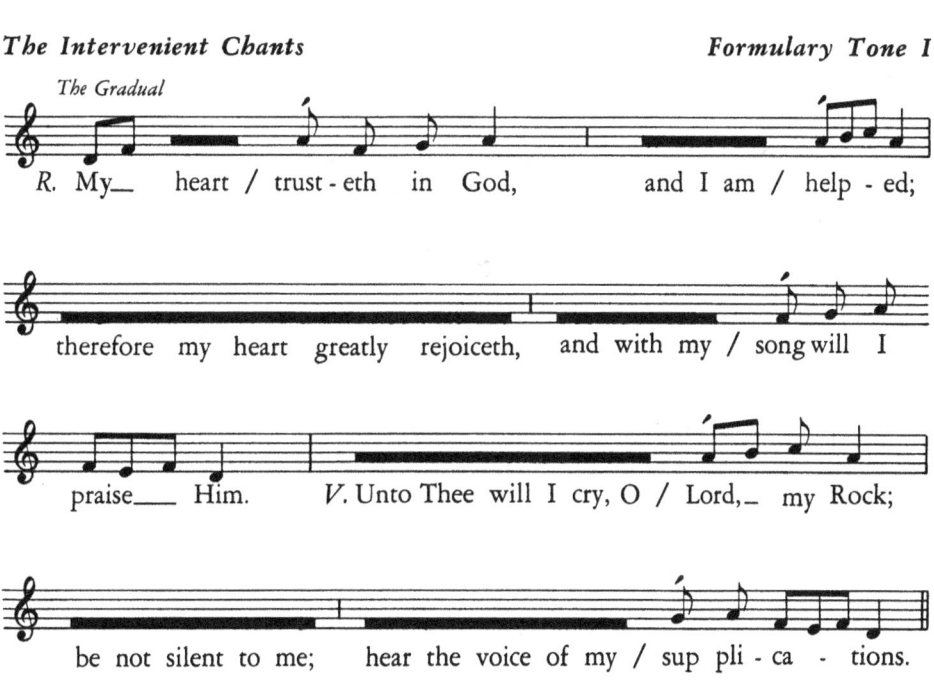

102

II

The Gloria Patri for the Introits of the Trinity Season, Cycle II

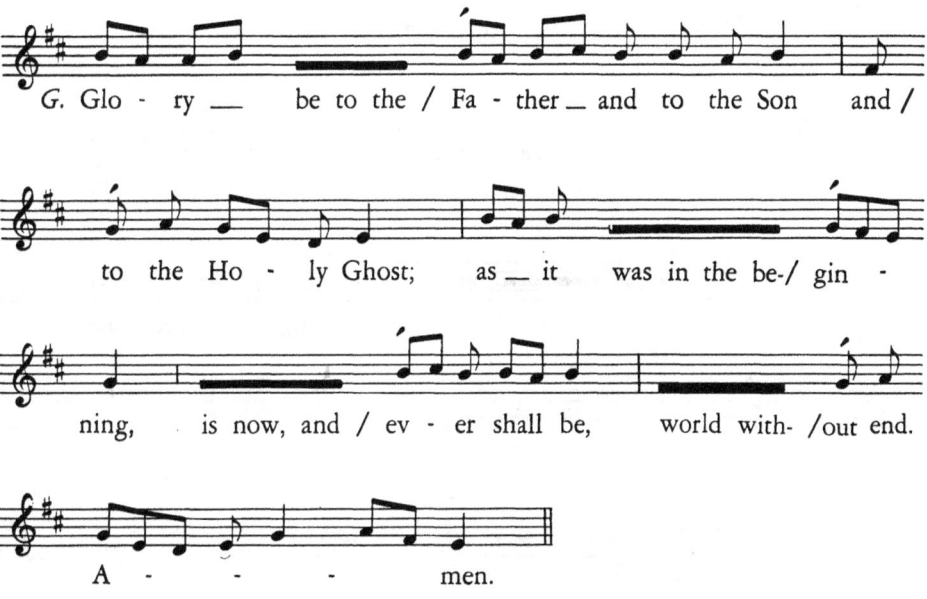

The Twelfth Sunday After Trinity

The Introit[1] *Formulary Tone V*

A.[2] Make haste, O God, to de-/ liv-er me; make haste to / help me, O Lord. Let them be ashamed and con / -found - ed that / seek af-ter my soul. Ps.[3] Let them be turned backward and put to con-/ fu - sion that de-/ sire my hurt. G.[4] Glo- ry be to the / Fa - ther and to the Son and / to the Ho- ly Ghost; as it was in the be-/ gin - ning, is now, and / ev- er shall be, world with-/ out end. A - - men.

A.[2] Make haste, O God, to de-/ liv - er me; make haste to / help me, O Lord. Let them be ashamed and con-/ found - ed that / seek af - ter my soul.

1. The complete form of the Introit is presented here as a model for the third cycle of the Trinity season. 2. Antiphon. 3. Psalmellus. 4. Gloria Patri.

105

The Intervenient Chants   *Formulary Tone VI*

1. Responsorium. 2. Versus. 3. The Alleluia is to be sung immediately upon the conclusion of the Gradual. 4. The jubilant Alleluias should, if at all possible, be sung in four parts (SATB); if not, the upper part may be sung in unison by the whole choir, or by an antiphonal junior or children's choir.

The Thirteenth Sunday After Trinity

The Introit — *Formulary Tone V*

A. Have respect, O Lord, unto Thy / covenant; oh, let not the oppressed re-/turn ashamed! Arise, O God, / plead Thine own cause; and forget not the / voice of Thine enemies.

Ps. O God, why hast Thou cast us off for-/ever? Why doth Thine anger smoke against the / sheep of Thy pasture?

Gloria Patri V, p. 115
Repeat Antiphon

The Intervenient Chants — *Formulary Tone VI*

The Gradual

R. Have respect, O Lord, unto Thy / covenant; oh, let not the oppressed re-/turn ashamed! V. Arise, O God, / plead Thine own cause, and forget not the / voice of Thine enemies.

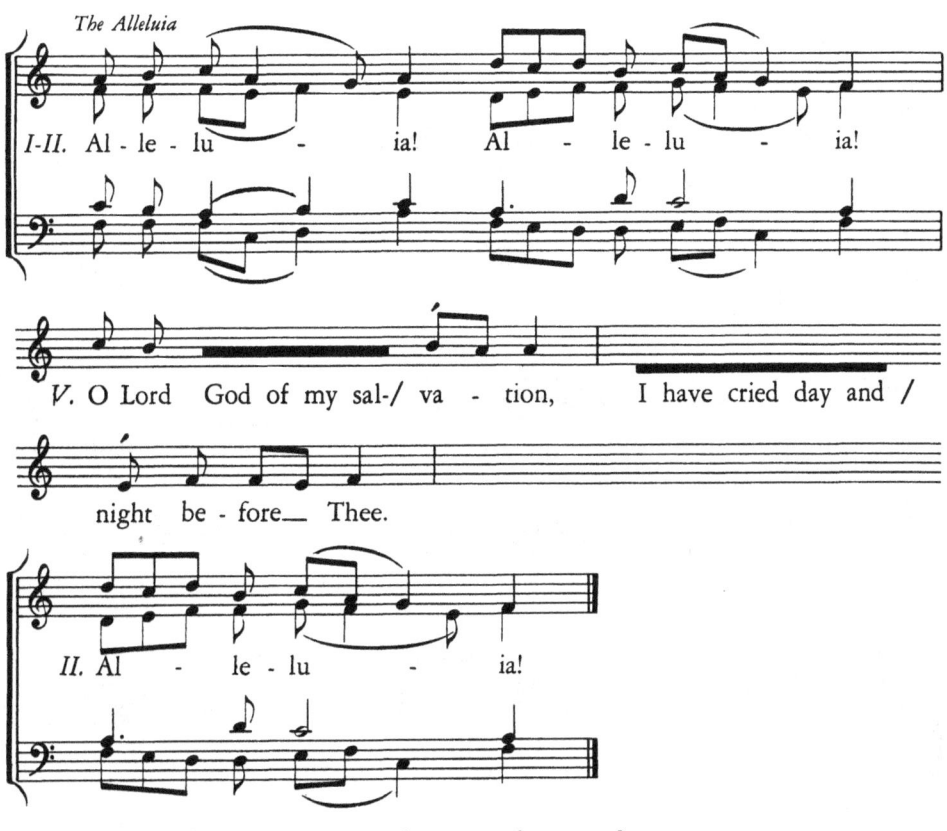

The Fourteenth Sunday After Trinity

The Introit   *Formulary Tone V*

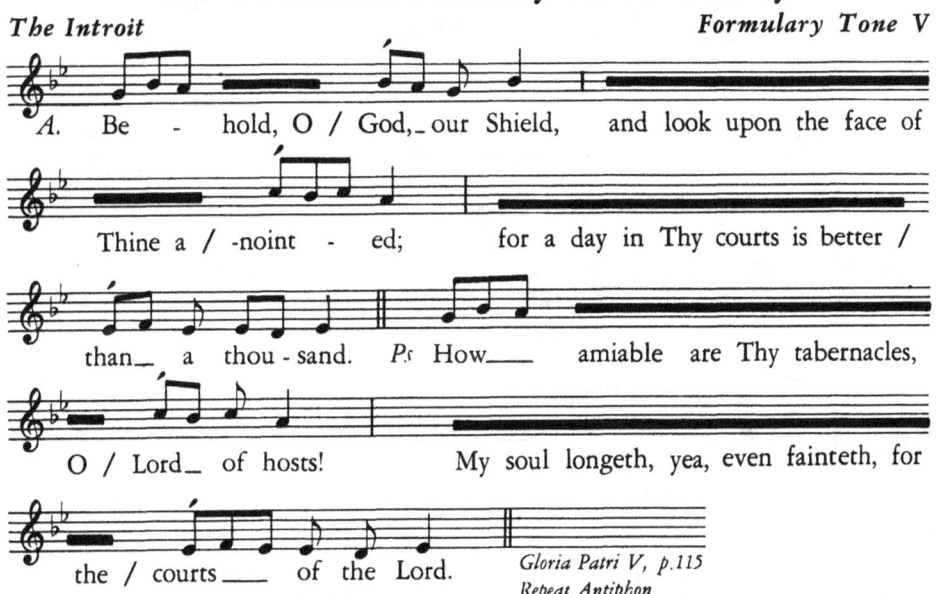

Gloria Patri V, p.115
Repeat Antiphon

108

The Intervenient Chants   *Formulary Tone VI*

The Gradual

R. It is a good thing to give thanks un-/ to the Lord and to sing praises unto Thy / name,— O Most High; V. To show forth Thy loving-kindness in the / morn - ing and Thy / faith-ful-ness ev - 'ry night.

The Alleluia

I-II. Al - le - lu - ia! Al - le - lu - ia!

V. Praise— waiteth for Thee, O God, in / Zi - on, and unto Thee shall the / vow be per - form - ed.

II. Al - le - lu - ia!

The Fifteenth Sunday After Trinity

The Introit   *Formulary Tone V*

A. Bow down Thine ear, O Lord, / hear me; O Thou, my God, save Thy servant that / trust-eth in Thee. Be merciful to / me, O Lord, for I cry / un-to Thee dai-ly.

Ps. Re-joice the soul of Thy / serv-ant; for unto Thee, O Lord, do I / lift up my soul. *Gloria Patri V, p.115*
Repeat Antiphon

The Intervenient Chants   *Formulary Tone VI*

The Gradual

R. It is better to / trust in the Lord than to put / con-fi-dence in man. V. It is better to / trust in the Lord than to put con-fi- / dence in princ-es.

The Alleluia

I-II. Al-le-lu-ia! Al-le-lu-ia!

The Sixteenth Sunday After Trinity

The Seventeenth Sunday After Trinity

The Introit — *Formulary Tone V*

A. Right-eous art Thou, / O Lord, and upright / are Thy judg-ments. Deal with Thy / serv - ant according / to Thy mer - cy. *Ps.* Bless-ed are the undefil-ed / in the way, who walk in the / Law of the Lord.

Gloria Patri V, p.115
Repeat Antiphon

The Intervenient Chants — *Formulary Tone VI*

The Gradual

R. Bless-ed is the nation whose / God is the Lord, and the people whom He hath chosen for His / own in-her-i-tance.

V. By the word of the Lord were the / heav-ens made, and all the host of them by the / breath of His mouth.

The Alleluia

I-II. Al-le-lu - ia! Al - le-lu - ia!

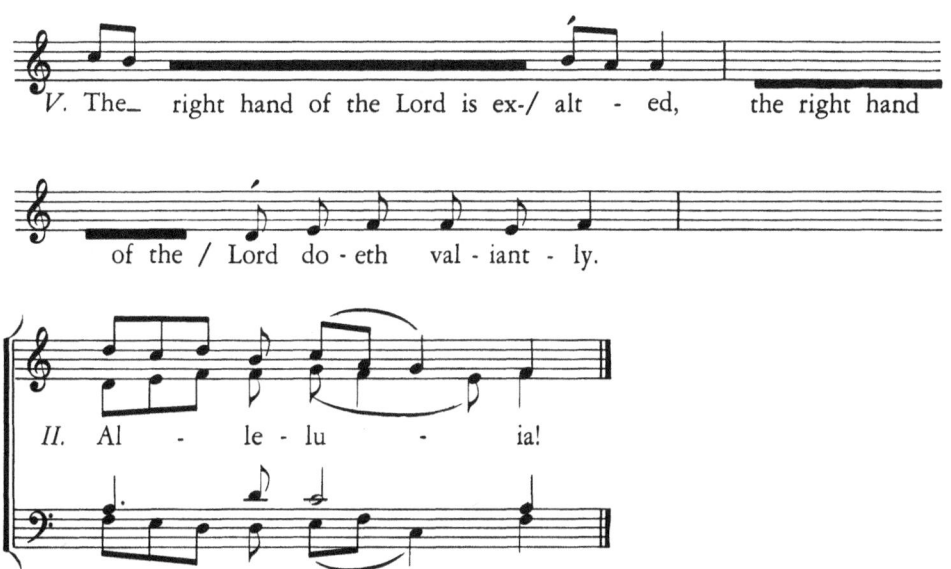

The Eighteenth Sunday After Trinity

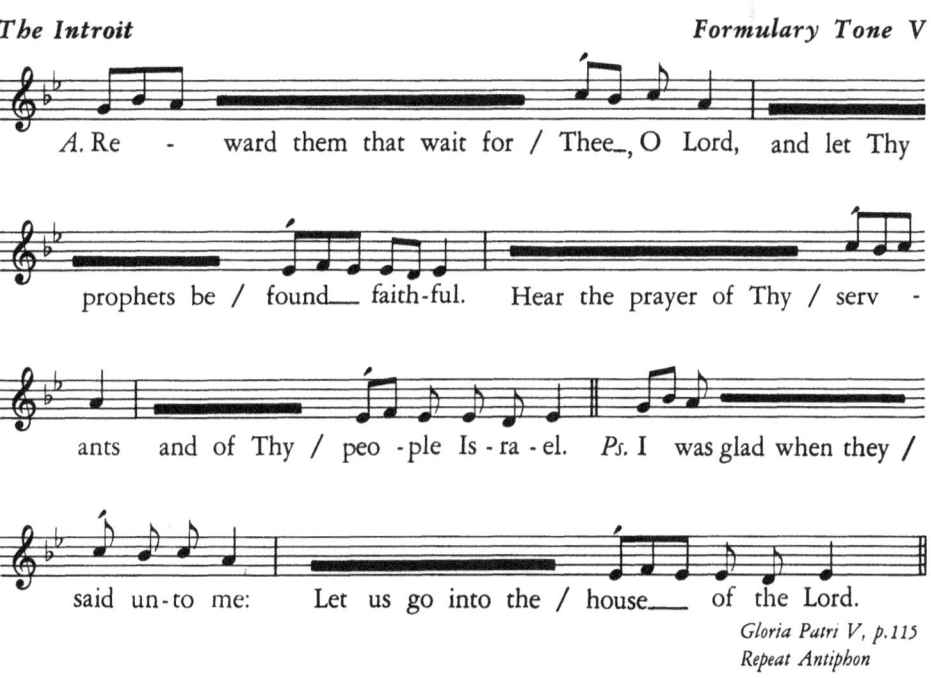

Gloria Patri V, p.115
Repeat Antiphon

The Intervenient Chants   *Formulary Tone VI*

V

The Gloria Patri for the Introits of the Trinity Season, Cycle III

116

The Nineteenth Sunday After Trinity

The Introit[1]   *Formulary Tone X*

A.[2] Say / unto my soul, I am / thy Salvation; the righteous cry, and the / Lord heareth. He delivereth them / out of their troubles; He is their God for-/ ever and ever. *Ps.*[3] Give ear, O My / people, to My Law; incline your / ears to the words of My mouth. *G.*[4] Glory be to the / Father and to the Son and / to the Holy Ghost; as it was in the be-/ ginning, is now, and / ever shall be, world with-/ out end. Amen. A.[2] Say / unto my soul, I am / thy Salvation, the righteous cry, and the / Lord heareth. He delivereth

117

them / out of their trou - bles; He is their God for-/ ev - er and ev - er.

1. The complete form of the Introit is presented here as a model for the fourth cycle of the Trinity season. 2. Antiphon. 3. Psalmellus. 4. Gloria Patri.

The Intervenient Chants   *Formulary Tone IX*

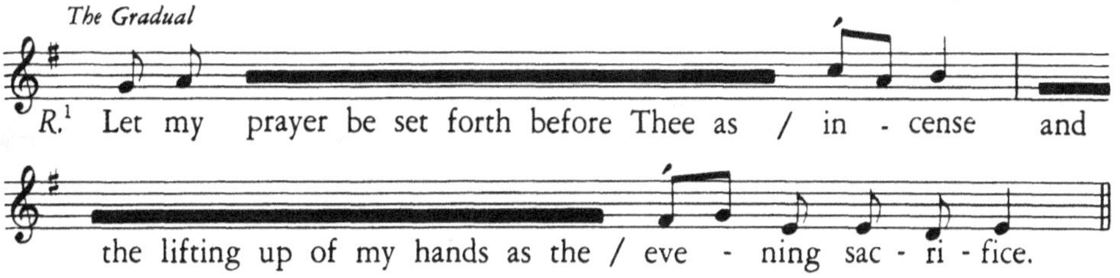

The Gradual

R.[1] Let my prayer be set forth before Thee as / in - cense and the lifting up of my hands as the / eve - ning sac - ri - fice.

The Alleluia[2]

Al - le - lu - ia!
I-II.[3] Al - le - lu - ia! Al - le - lu - ia!
Al - le - lu - ia!

V.[4] Oh,— sing unto the Lord a / new— song, for / He hath done mar - v'lous things.

Al - le - lu - ia!
II.[3] Al - le - lu - ia!
Al - le - lu - ia!

1. Responsorium. 2. The Alleluia is to be sung immediately upon the conclusion of the Gradual. 3. The jubilant Alleluias should, if at all possible, be sung in four parts (SATB); if not, the upper part may be sung in unison by the whole choir, or by an antiphonal junior or children's choir. 4. Versus.

120

The Intervenient Chants   *Formulary Tone IX*

The Twenty-second Sunday After Trinity

The Introit — *Formulary Tone X*

A. If Thou, Lord, shouldest / mark in-iq-ui-ties, O / Lord, who shall stand? But there is for-/ give-ness with Thee, that Thou mayest be feared, O / God of Is-ra-el. *Ps.* Out of the depths have I / cried un-to Thee, O Lord; Lord hear my voice.

Gloria Patri X, p. 131
Repeat Antiphon

The Intervenient Chants — *Formulary Tone IX*

The Gradual

R. Be-hold how good and how / pleas-ant it is for brethren to dwell to-/ geth-er in u-ni-ty! V. The Lord commanded / bless-ing, even / life for-ev-er-more.

The Alleluia

I-II. Al-le-lu-ia! Al-le-lu-ia! Al-le-lu-ia! Al-le-lu-ia!

V. The Lord healeth the / bro-ken in heart and / bind-eth up their wounds.

The Twenty-third Sunday After Trinity

The Introit   *Formulary Tone X*

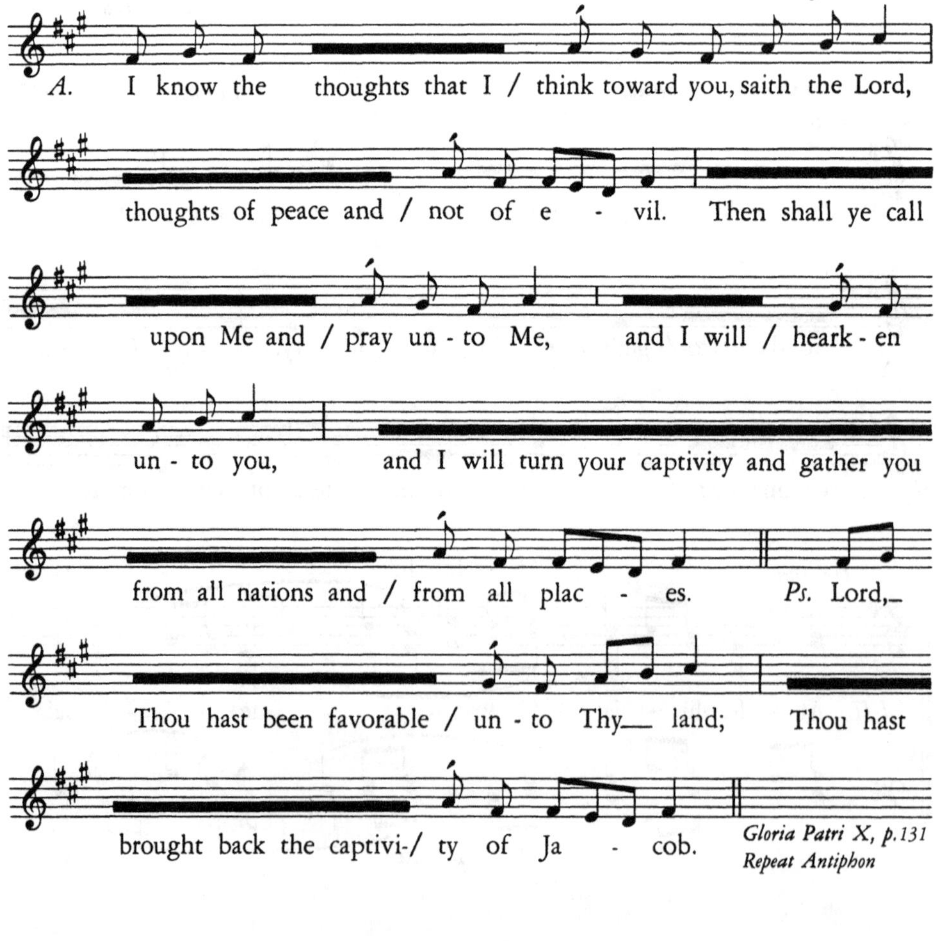

A. I know the thoughts that I / think toward you, saith the Lord, thoughts of peace and / not of e - vil. Then shall ye call upon Me and / pray un-to Me, and I will / heark-en un-to you, and I will turn your captivity and gather you from all nations and / from all plac - es. *Ps.* Lord, Thou hast been favorable / un-to Thy land; Thou hast brought back the captivi-/ ty of Ja - cob.

Gloria Patri X, p.131
Repeat Antiphon

The Twenty-fourth Sunday After Trinity

The Introit *Formulary Tone X*

A. Oh, come, let us / wor-ship and bow down; let us kneel before the / Lord, our Mak - er. For / He is our God, and we are the people of His pasture and the / sheep of His hand. *Ps.* Oh, come, let us / sing un-to the Lord; let us make a joyful noise to the Rock of / our sal - va - tion. *Gloria Patri X, p. 131* *Repeat Antiphon*

The Intervenient Chants *Formulary Tone IX*

The Gradual

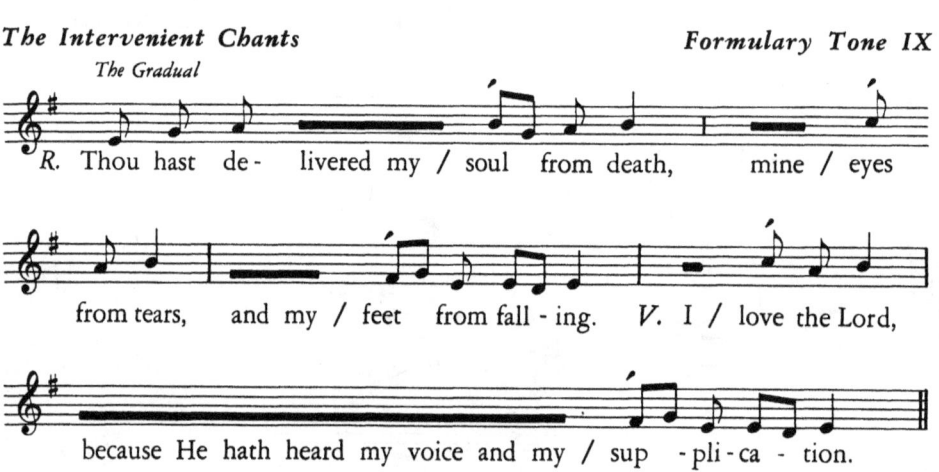

R. Thou hast de-livered my / soul from death, mine / eyes from tears, and my / feet from fall - ing. V. I / love the Lord, because He hath heard my voice and my / sup - pli-ca - tion.

The Twenty-fifth Sunday After Trinity

126

Ps. In Thee, O / Lord, do I put my trust; let me / never be a-shamed. *Gloria Patri X, p.131* / *Repeat Antiphon*

The Intervenient Chants   *Formulary Tone IX*

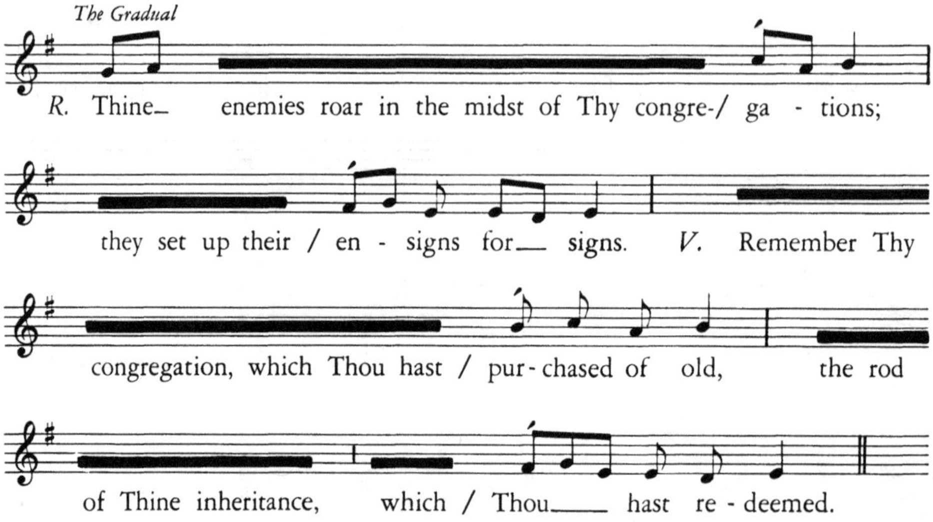

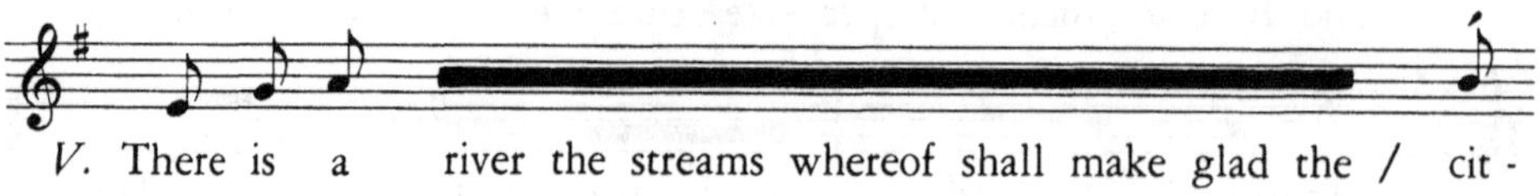

The Gradual

R. Thine enemies roar in the midst of Thy congre-/ ga - tions; they set up their / en - signs for signs. V. Remember Thy congregation, which Thou hast / pur-chased of old, the rod of Thine inheritance, which / Thou hast re-deemed.

The Alleluia

I-II. Al - le-lu - ia! Al - le-lu - ia! Al - le-lu - ia! Al - le-lu - ia!

V. There is a river the streams whereof shall make glad the / cit-

The Twenty-sixth Sunday After Trinity

The Twenty-seventh Sunday After Trinity

The Introit *Formulary Tone X*

(The Introit for the Twenty-third Sunday after Trinity shall be used on the last Sunday after Trinity in each year, p. 122)

The Intervenient Chants *Formulary Tone IX*

The Gradual

R. The King's daughter shall be brought un-/ to the King; the virgins, her companions that follow her, shall be / brought un-to Thee. V. With gladness and rejoicing / shall they be brought; they shall enter into the / King's pal-ace.

The Alleluia

Al-le-lu-ia! I-II. Al-le-lu-ia! Al-le-lu-ia! Al-le-lu-ia!

V. I saw the holy city, New Je-/ ru-sa-lem, coming down

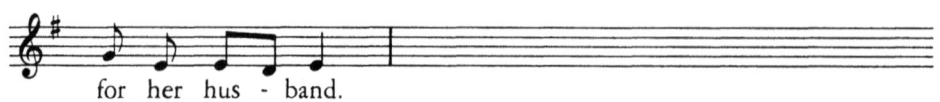

X

The Gloria Patri for the Introits of the Trinity Season, Cycle IV

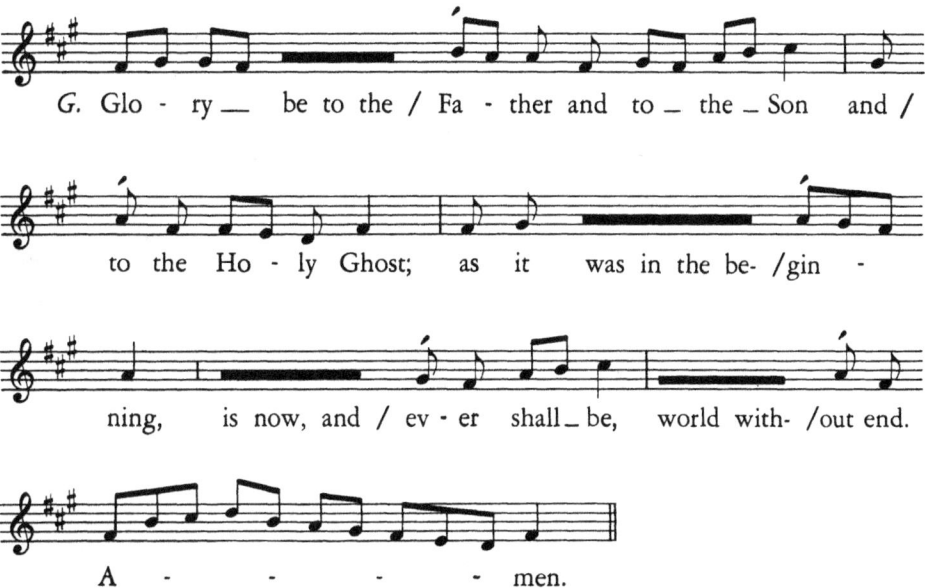

The
Introits and
Intervenient Chants
for the
Occasions

The Festival of Harvest

The Introit — *Formulary Tone XI*

A. O Lord, Thou crownest the year with Thy / goodness, and Thy / paths drop fatness. Thou visitest the earth and / waterest it; Thou / blessest the springing thereof.

Ps. Praise waiteth for Thee, O God, in / Zion, and unto Thee shall the / vow be performed.

Gloria Patri XI, p.19
Repeat Antiphon

The Intervenient Chants — *Formulary Tone XII*

The Gradual

R. The eyes of all / wait upon Thee, and Thou givest them their / meat in due season. V. Thou / openest Thine hand and satisfiest the desire of / ev'ry living thing.

The Alleluia

I-II. Alleluia! Alleluia! Alleluia!

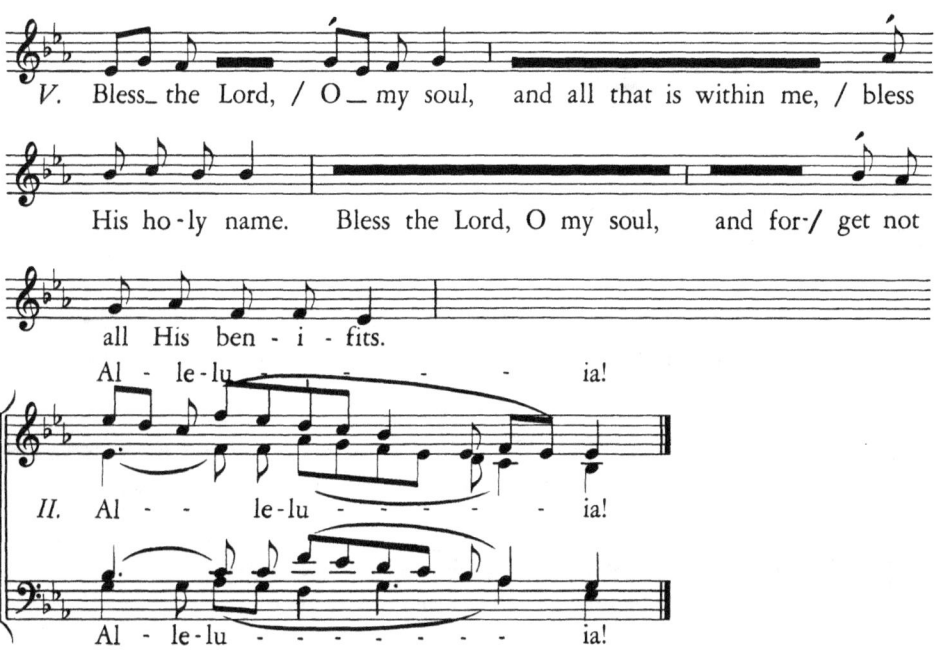

The Festival of the Reformation

The Introit *Formulary Tone VII*

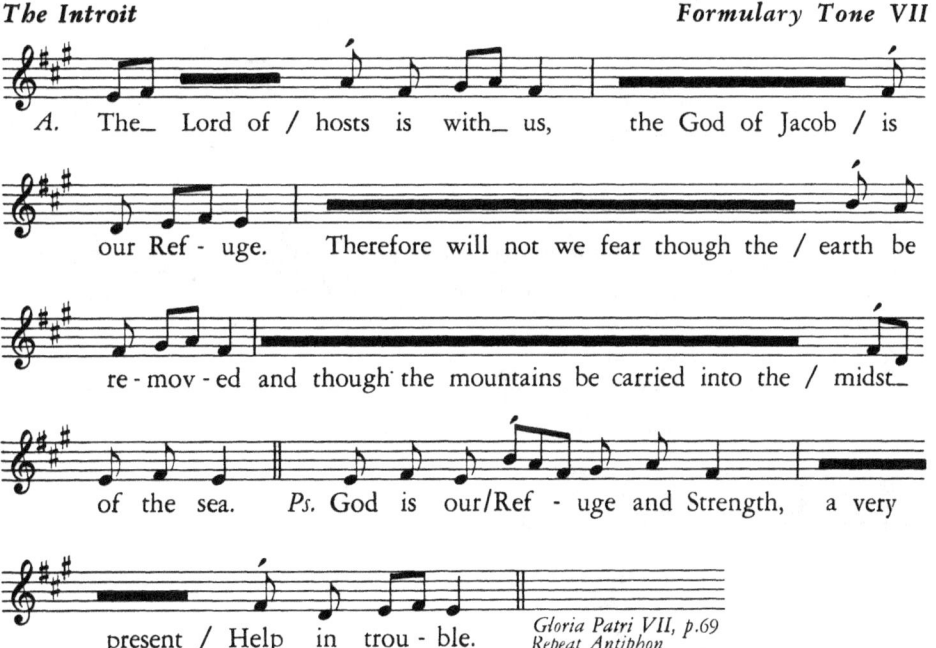

A. The Lord of / hosts is with us, the God of Jacob / is our Ref - uge. Therefore will not we fear though the / earth be re - mov - ed and though the mountains be carried into the / midst of the sea. *Ps.* God is our / Ref - uge and Strength, a very present / Help in trou - ble.

Gloria Patri VII, p.69
Repeat Antiphon

The Intervenient Chants
Formulary Tone VIII

A Day of Humiliation and Prayer

The Introit   *Formulary Tone I*

A. Hear, O heavens, and give / ear, O earth, for the Lord hath / spo - ken: I have nourished and brought up children, and they have re-/ belled a - gainst Me. They have for-/ sak - en the Lord, they have provoked the Holy One of Israel unto / an - ger; they are / gone a - way back - ward. *Ps.* If Thou, Lord, shouldest mark in-/ iq - ui -ties, O / Lord, who shall stand?

Repeat Antiphon[1]

1. On this day the Gloria Patri is omitted.

The Intervenient Chant   *Formulary Tone II*

The Tract

Tr. Seek ye the Lord while / He may be found, call ye up-/ on Him while He is near. V. Let the / wick - ed for - sake his way and the un-/ right - eous man his thoughts. V. And let

him return un-/ to the Lord, and He will have / mer-cy up-on him, and to our God, for He will a-/ bun-dant-ly par - don.

A Day of General or Special Thanksgiving

The Introit — *Formulary Tone XI*

A. Let everything that hath breath / praise the Lord; praise ye the Lord. Praise Him for His / might - y acts, praise Him according to His / ex - cel-lent great - ness. *Ps.* Praise /ye the Lord, praise God in His sanctu-/ ar - y, praise Him in the / fir - ma-ment of His pow'r. *Gloria Patri XI, p.19*
Repeat Antiphon

The Intervenient Chants — *Formulary Tone XII*

(*The Gradual and the Alleluia are the same as for the Festival of Harvest, p. 134*).

The Presentation of Our Lord and the Purification of Mary

The Introit — *Formulary Tone II*
(*The Introit is the same as for the Eighth Sunday after Trinity, p. 96*).

The Introit (alternate) — *Formulary Tone IX*

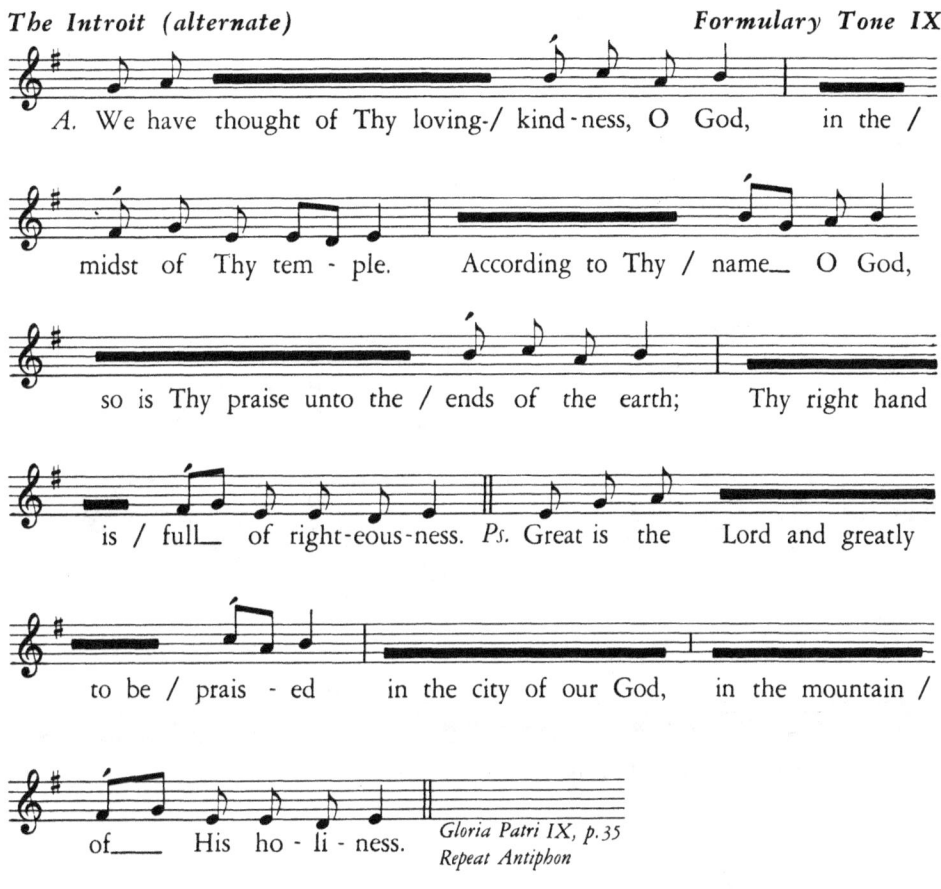

A. We have thought of Thy loving-/ kind-ness, O God, in the / midst of Thy tem-ple. According to Thy / name O God, so is Thy praise unto the / ends of the earth; Thy right hand is / full of right-eous-ness. *Ps.* Great is the Lord and greatly to be / prais-ed in the city of our God, in the mountain / of His ho-li-ness. *Gloria Patri IX, p.35* *Repeat Antiphon*

The Intervenient Chants — *Formulary Tone 1*

The Gradual

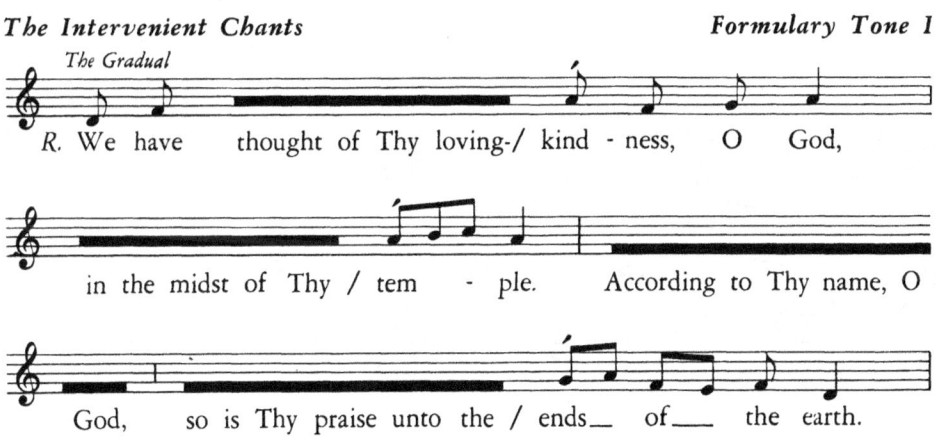

R. We have thought of Thy loving-/ kind-ness, O God, in the midst of Thy / tem - ple. According to Thy name, O God, so is Thy praise unto the / ends of the earth.

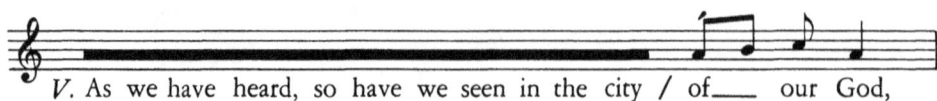

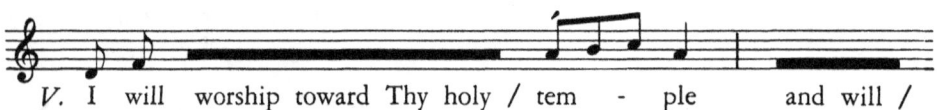
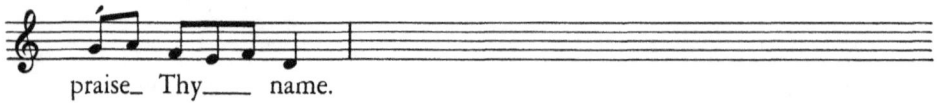

141

The Intervenient Chants (alternate) [1]   *Formulary Tone* X

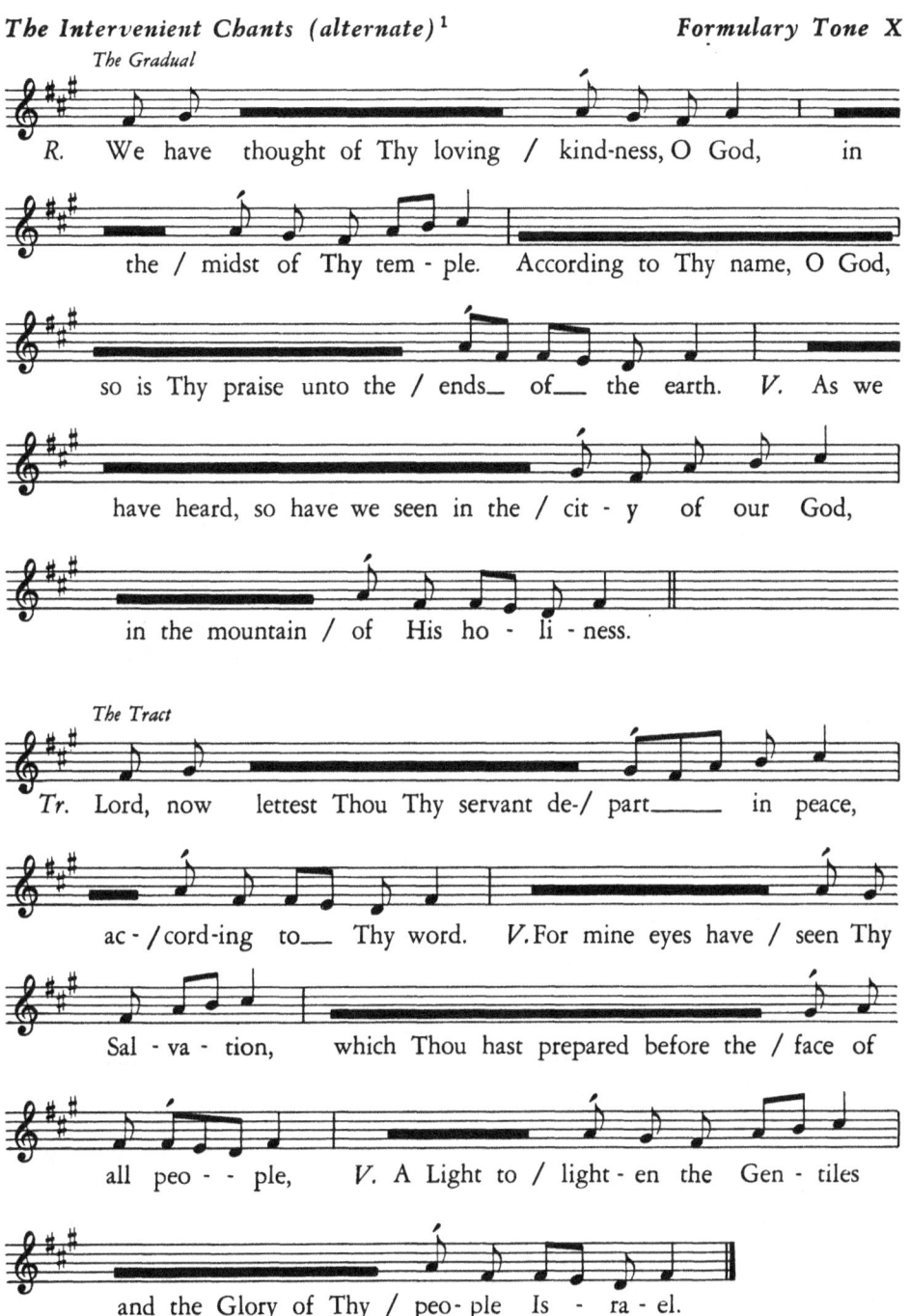

1. If this festival falls after Septuagesima, the alternate Gradual and Tract are used.

The Annunciation

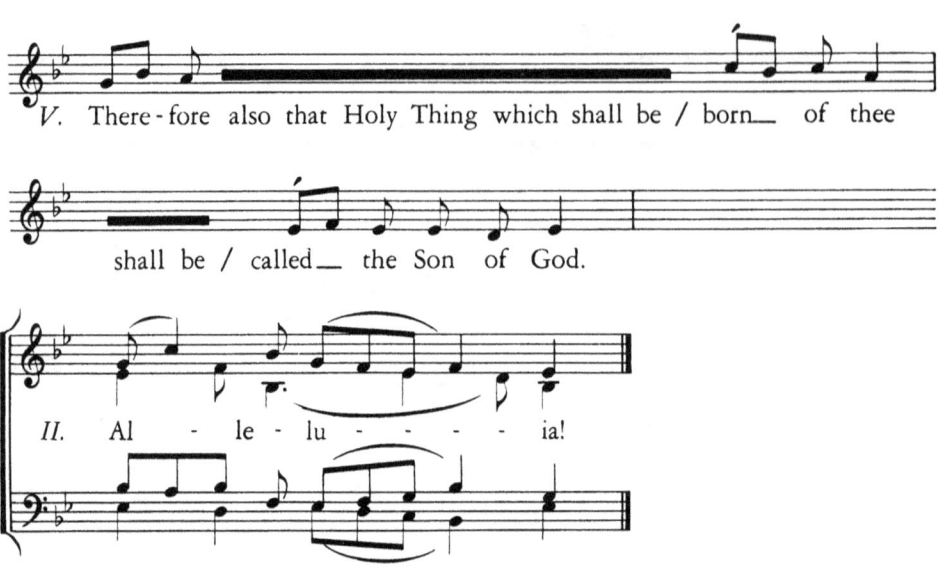

The Visitation

The Introit Formulary Tone VI

(*The Introit is the same as for the Annunciation, p. 142*)

The Intervenient Chants Formulary Tone V
The Gradual

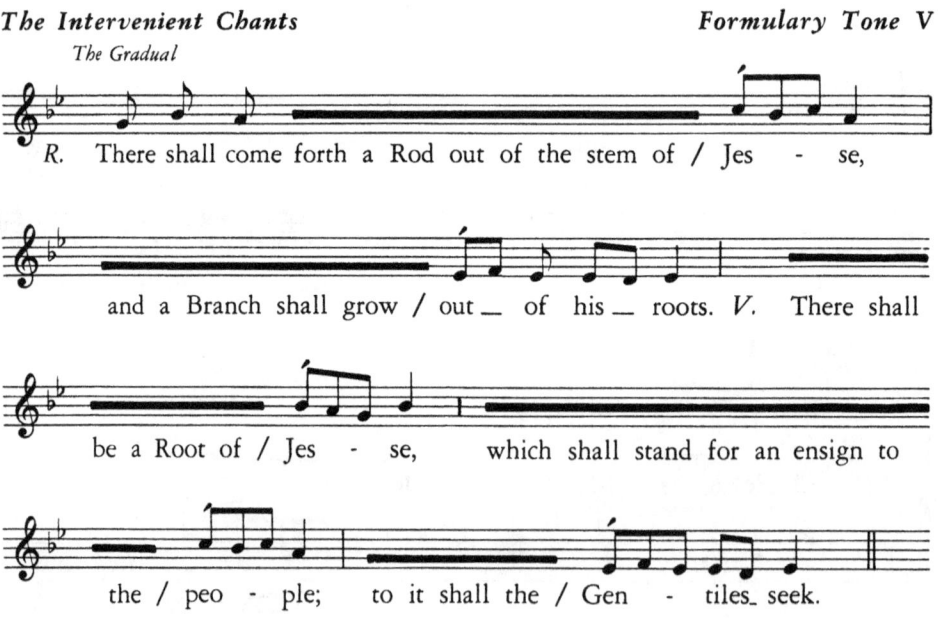

The Alleluia

I-II. Alleluia! Alleluia!

V. Blessed art thou, O Mary, among / women, and blessed is the / fruit of thy womb; behold, there shall be a performance of those things which were / told thee from the Lord.

II. Alleluia!

Evangelists', Apostles', and Martyrs' Days

The Introit Evangelists' Days *Formulary Tone XI*

A. The Lord God / said unto me: Write all the words that I have spoken unto thee into a / book for a memo-

146

rial. *Ps.* His name shall endure for-/ ev - - er; His name shall be con-/ tin-ued as long as the sun. *Gloria Patri XI, p. 19* *Repeat Antiphon*

The Intervenient Chants   *Formulary Tone XII*

The Gradual

R. Thou art fairer than the / chil-dren of men; grace is / poured in-to Thy lips. *V* My heart is inditing a / good mat - ter; I speak of the things which I have / made touch - ing the King.

The Alleluia

Al - le-lu - - - - - - - ia!
I-II. Al - le-lu - ia! Al - - - le-lu - - - - - - ia!
Al - le-lu - - - - - - - - ia!

V. The Lord Jesus gave some, apostles, and / some, e-van-gelists   for the edifying / of the bo - dy of Christ.

Al - le - lu - - - - ia!
II. Al - - - le - lu - - - - ia!
Al - le - lu - - - - - ia!

The Intervenient Chants (alternate)   Formulary Tone XII

The Gradual

R. How___ beautiful are the good tidings of him that / pub-lish-eth___ peace,   that saith unto / Zi - on: Thy God reign - eth!

V. The Lord hath made bare His holy arm in the / eyes of all na-tions;   and all the ends of the earth shall see the sal-/ va-tion of our God.

The Alleluia

Al - le - lu - - - - ia!
I-II. Al - le - lu - ia! Al - - le - lu - - - - ia!
Al - le - lu - - - - - ia!

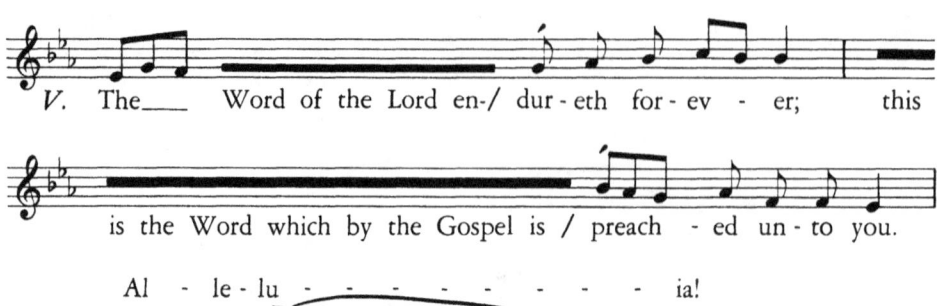

V. The Word of the Lord en-/ dur-eth for-ev-er; this is the Word which by the Gospel is / preach-ed un-to you.

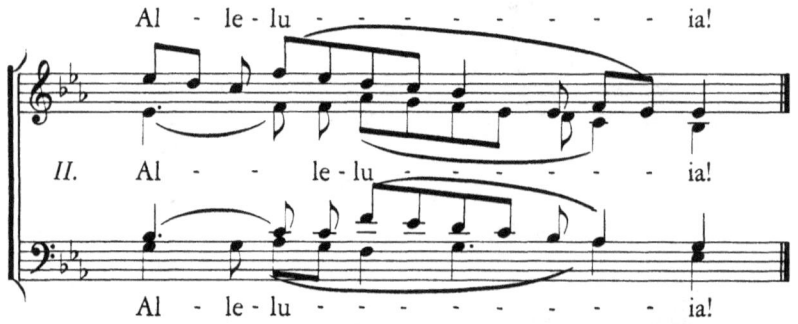

Al-le-lu - - - - - ia!
II. Al - le-lu - - - - - ia!
Al-le-lu - - - - - - ia!

Apostles' Days

The Introit *Formulary Tone VII*

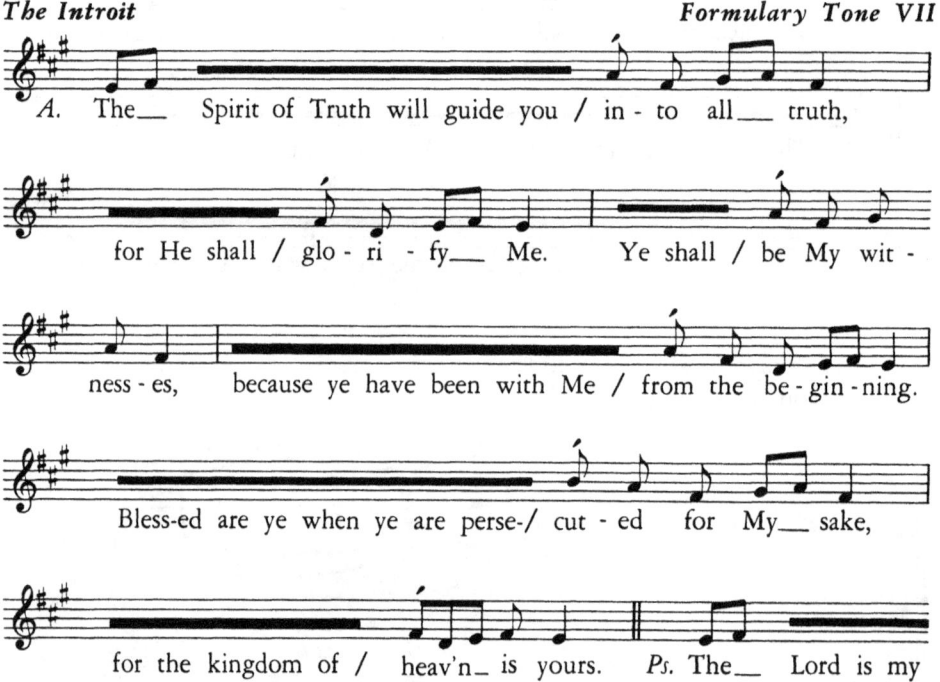

A. The Spirit of Truth will guide you / in-to all truth, for He shall / glo-ri-fy Me. Ye shall / be My wit-ness-es, because ye have been with Me / from the be-gin-ning. Bless-ed are ye when ye are perse-/ cut-ed for My sake, for the kingdom of / heav'n is yours. *Ps.* The Lord is my

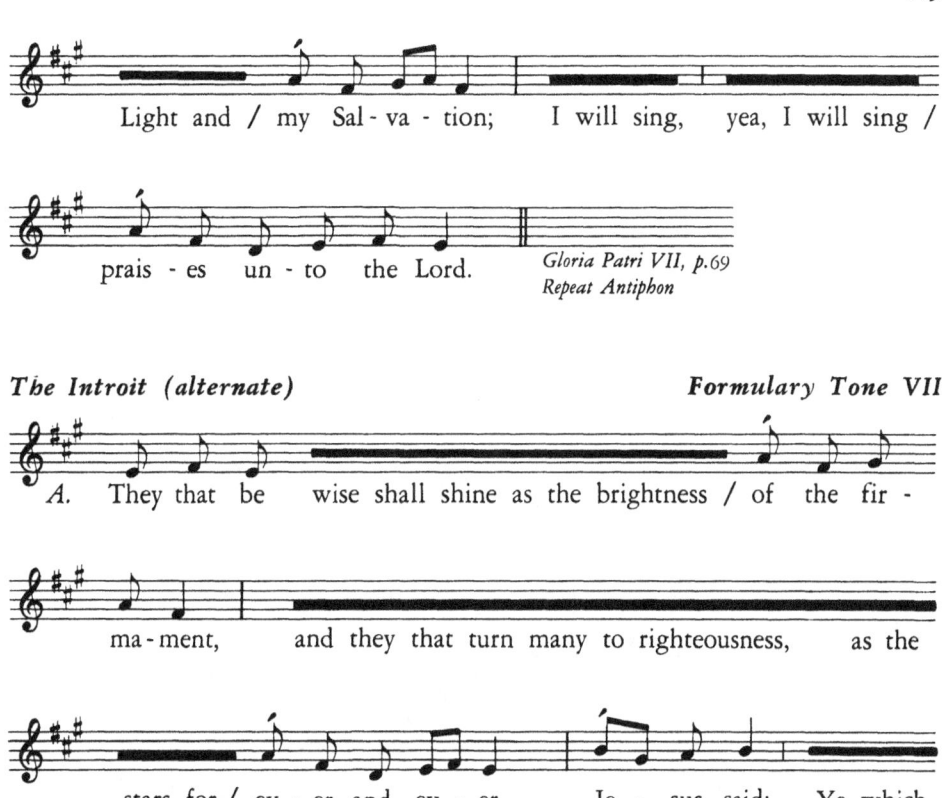
Light and / my Sal-va-tion; I will sing, yea, I will sing / prais-es un-to the Lord.

Gloria Patri VII, p.69
Repeat Antiphon

The Introit (alternate)   *Formulary Tone VII*

A. They that be wise shall shine as the brightness / of the fir-ma-ment, and they that turn many to righteousness, as the stars for-/ ev-er and ev-er. Je-sus said: Ye which have followed Me, in the re-/ gen-er-a-tion, when the Son of Man shall sit in the throne of His glory, ye also shall / sit up-on twelve thrones. *Ps.* I will bless the / Lord at all times; His praise shall continually / be in my mouth.

Gloria Patri VII, p.69
Repeat Antiphon

152

Ps. O Lord, Thou hast searched me and / known me; Thou knowest my downsitting and / mine up-ris-ing.

Gloria Patri IX, p.35
Repeat Antiphon

The Intervenient Chants *Formulary Tone X*

The Gradual

R. The mouth of the righteous / speak-eth of wis-dom, and his tongue / talk-eth of judg-ment. V. The Law of his / God is in his heart; none of his steps shall slide.

The Alleluia

I-II. Alleluia! Alleluia! Alleluia! Alleluia!

V. The righteous shall flourish / like the palm tree; those that be planted in the house of the Lord shall flourish in the / courts of our God.

Saint Thomas the Apostle's Day

The Introit *Formulary Tone VII*

(The Introit is the same as for Evangelists', Apostles', and Martyrs' Days, p. 148)

The Intervenient Chants *Formulary Tone VIII*

(The Gradual and the Alleluia are the same as for Evangelists', Apostles', and Martyrs' Days, p. 150)

Saint Stephen the Martyr's Day

The Introit *Formulary Tone IX*

Gloria Patri IX, p.35
Repeat Antiphon

154

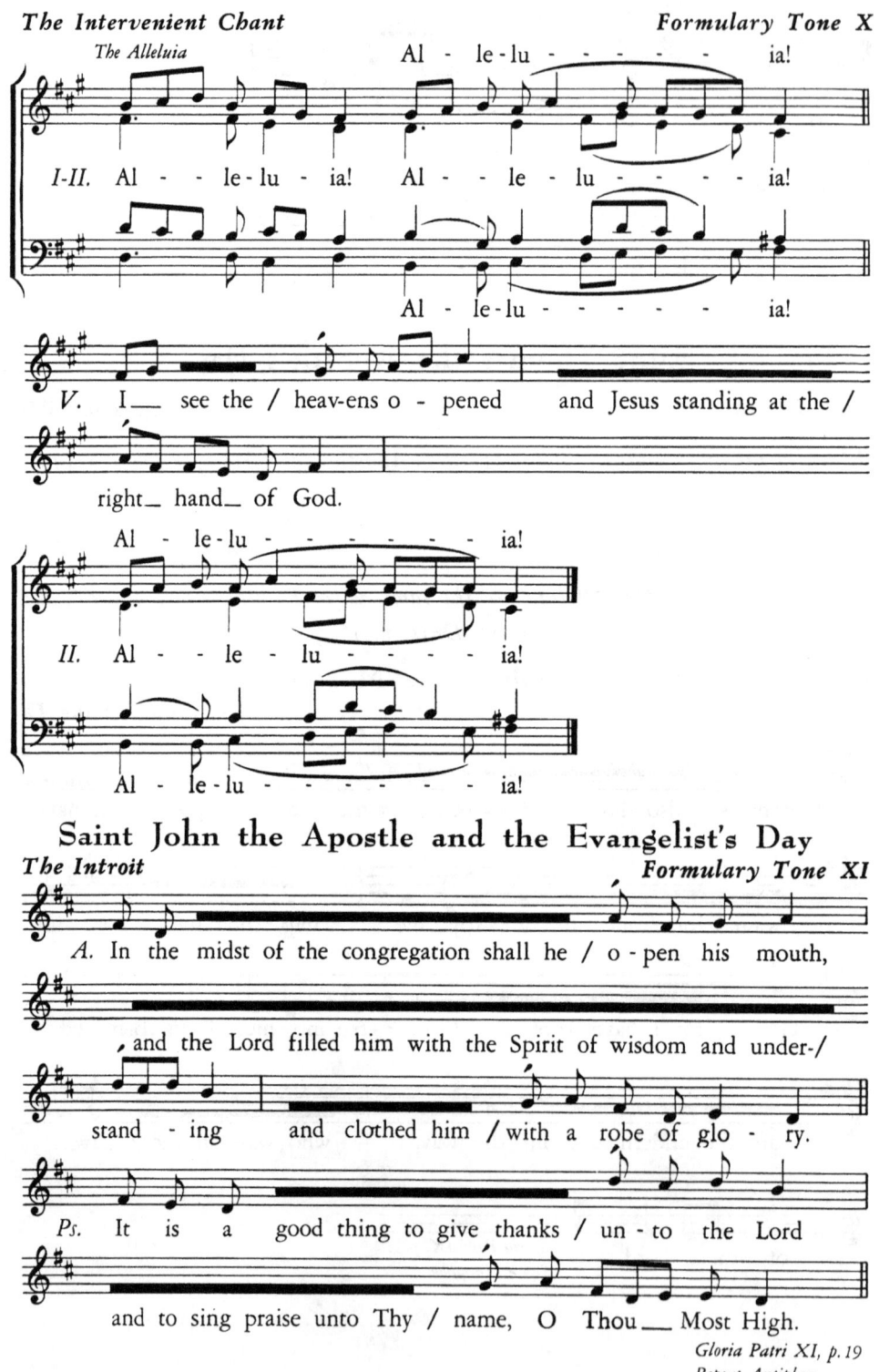

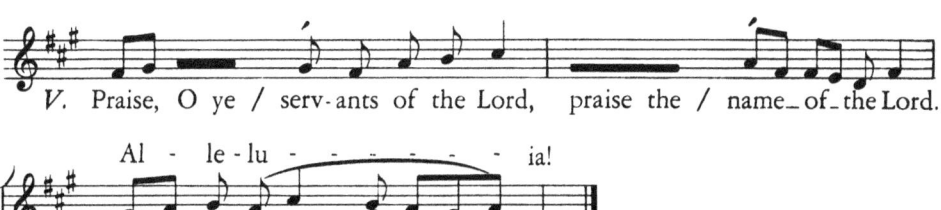

The Conversion of Saint Paul

The Introit   *Formulary Tone VII*

(*The Introit is the same as for Evangelists', Apostles', and Martyrs' Days, p. 148*)

The Intervenient Chants   *Formulary Tone VIII*

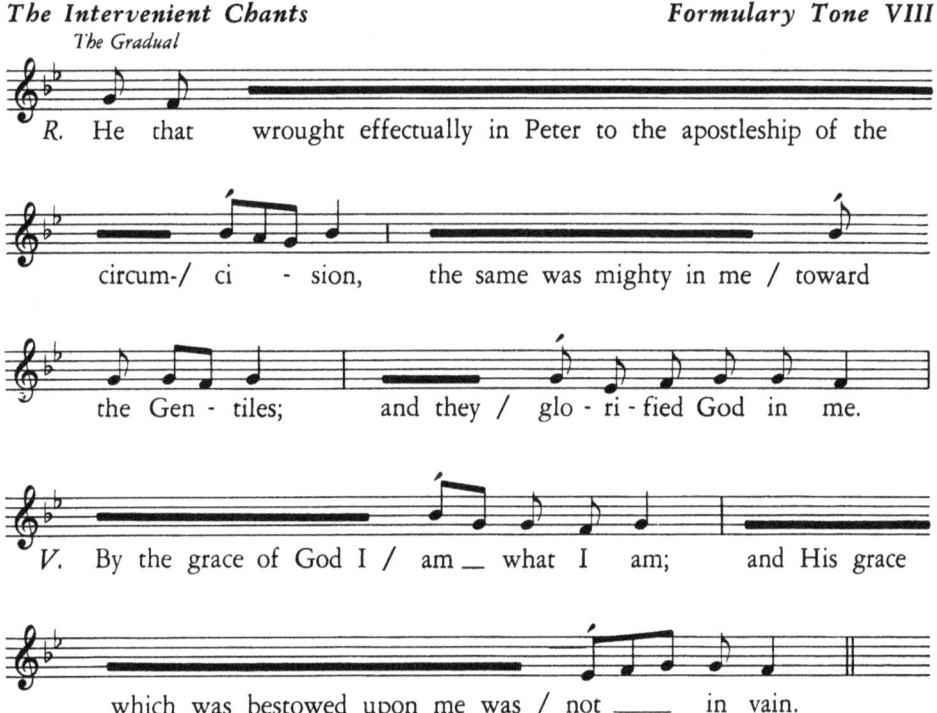

158

The Alleluia

I-II. Alleluia! Alleluia!

V. The Lord / said unto Paul: Thou art a chosen / vessel unto Me to bear My name be-/ fore the Gentiles.

II. Alleluia!

Saint Matthias the Apostle's Day

The Introit **Formulary Tone VII**

(*The Introit is the same as for Evangelists', Apostles', and Martyrs' Days, p. 148*)

The Intervenient Chants **Formulary Tone VIII**

(*The Gradual and the Alleluia, or the Alleluia, are the same as for Evangelists', Apostles', and Martyrs' Days, p. 150*)

Saint Mark the Evangelist's Day

The Introit **Formulary Tone XI**

(*The Introit is the same as for Evangelists', Apostles', and Martyrs' Days, p. 145*)

The Intervenient Chants **Formulary Tone XII**

(*The Gradual and the Alleluia, or the Alleluia, are the same as for Evangelists', Apostles', and Martyrs' Days, p. 146*)

Saint Philip and Saint James the Apostles' Day

The Introit   *Formulary Tone VII*

(*The Introit is the same as for Evangelists', Apostles', and Martyrs' Days, p. 148*)

The Intervenient Chants   *Formulary Tone VIII*

(*The Gradual and the Alleluia, or the Alleluia, are the same as for Evangelists', Apostles', and Martyrs' Days, p. 150*)

The Nativity of Saint John the Baptist

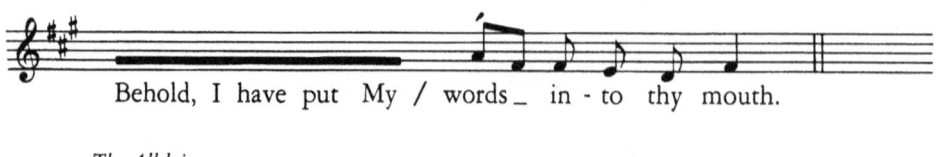

Saint Peter and Saint Paul the Apostles' Day

The Introit   *Formulary Tone VII*
(*The Introit is the same as for Evangelists', Apostles', and Martyrs' Days, p. 148*)

The Intervenient Chants   *Formulary Tone VIII*

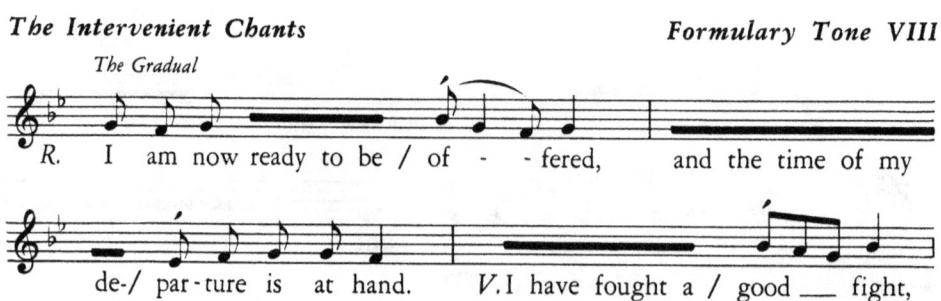

I have / fin-ished my course, I have / kept the faith.

The Alleluia

I-II. Al-le-lu-ia! Al-le-lu-ia!

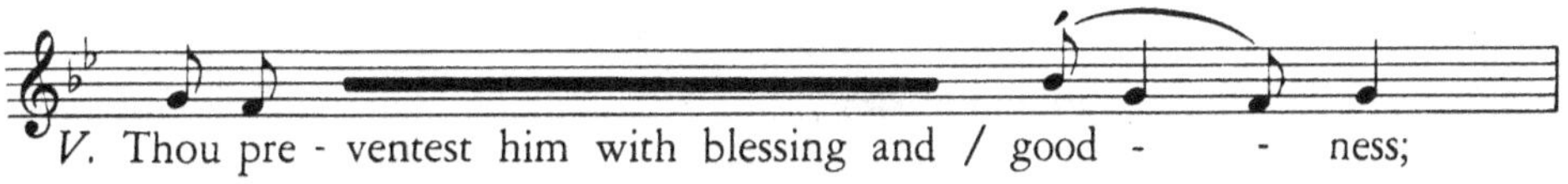

V. Thou pre-ventest him with blessing and / good-ness; Thou settest a crown of pure / gold on his head.

II. Al-le-lu-ia!

Saint Mary Magdalene's Day

The Introit — *Formulary Tone I*

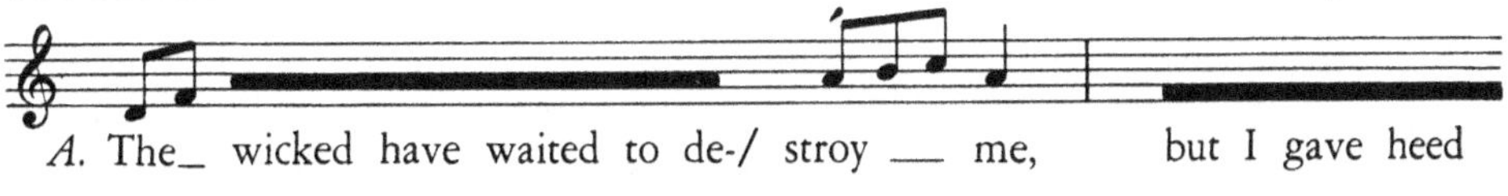

A. The wicked have waited to de-/stroy me, but I gave heed unto Thy / tes-ti-mo-nies. I have seen an end of all per-/

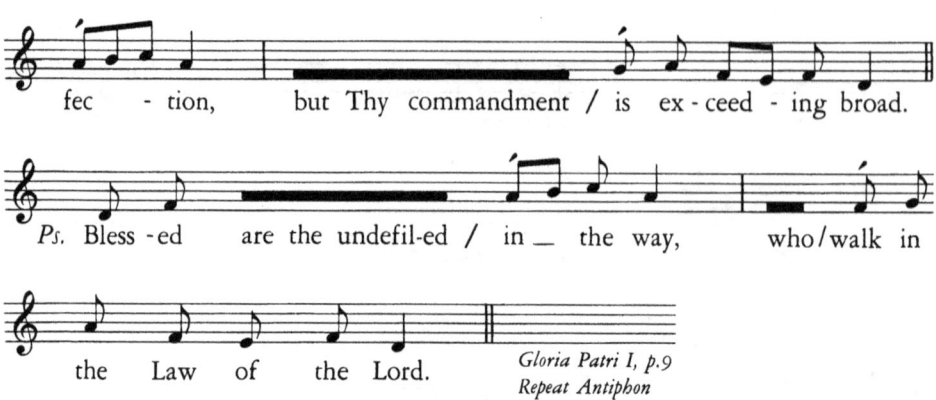

Saint James the Elder the Apostle's Day

The Introit   *Formulary Tone VII*

(*The Introit, or alternate, is the same as for Evangelists', Apostles', and Martyrs' Days, p. 148*)

The Intervenient Chants   *Formulary Tone VIII*

(*The Gradual and the Alleluia, or the Alleluia, are the same as for Evangelists', Apostles', and Martyrs' Days, p. 150*)

Saint Bartholomew the Apostle's Day

The Introit   *Formulary Tone VII*

(*The Introit, or alternate, is the same as for Evangelists', Apostles', and Martyrs' Days, p. 148*)

The Intervenient Chants   *Formulary Tone VIII*

(*The Gradual and the Alleluia, or the Alleluia, are the same as for Evangelists', Apostles', and Martyrs' Days, p. 150*)

164

Saint Matthew the Apostle and the Evangelist's Day

The Introit   *Formulary Tone XI*

(The Introit is the same as for Evangelists', Apostles', and Martyrs' Days, p. 145)

The Intervenient Chants   *Formulary Tone XII*

(The Gradual and the Alleluia, or alternate, are the same as for Evangelists', Apostles', and Martyrs' Days, p. 146)

Saint Michael's and All Angels' Day

The Introit   *Formulary Tone I*

A. Bless the Lord, ye His angels, that ex-/ cel __ in strength, that do His com-/ mand - ments, hearkening unto the / voice __ of __ His word. Bless ye the Lord, all / ye __ His hosts, ye ministers of His that / do His pleas - ure. Ps. Bless the Lord, / O __ my soul, and all that is within me, / bless His ho - ly name. *Gloria Patri I, p.9 Repeat Antiphon*

The Intervenient Chants   *Formulary Tone II*
The Gradual

R. God hath given His angels / charge __ o - ver thee to / keep thee in all __ thy ways. V. Bless the / Lord, __ O my soul, and all that is within me, / bless His ho - ly name.

Saint Luke the Evangelist's Day

The Introit   *Formulary Tone XI*
(*The Introit is the same as for Evangelists', Apostles', and Martyrs' Days, p. 145*)

The Intervenient Chants   *Formulary Tone XII*
(*The Gradual and the Alleluia, or alternate, are the same as for Evangelists',
Apostles', and Martyrs' Days, p. 146*)

Saint Simon and Saint Jude the Apostles' Day

The Introit   *Formulary Tone VII*
(*The Introit, or alternate, is the same as for Evangelists', Apostles', and Martyrs'
Days, p. 148*)

166

The Intervenient Chants *Formulary Tone VIII*
(*The Gradual and the Alleluia, or the Alleluia, are the same as for Evangelists', Apostles', and Martyrs' Days, p. 150*)

All Saints' Day

The Introit *Formulary Tone I*

A. A great multitude which no man could / num - - ber stood before the throne and be-/ fore the Lamb, clothed with white robes and with / palms in their hands; and cried with a loud voice, / say - ing: Salvation to our God, which sitteth upon the / throne, and un - to the Lamb. Ps. Re - joice in the Lord, O ye / right - eous, for praise is comely / for the up - right.

Gloria Patri I, p. 9
Repeat Antiphon

The Intervenient Chants *Formulary Tone II*
The Gradual

R. Oh, fear the / Lord, ye His saints, for there is no want to / them that fear Him. V. They that / seek the Lord shall not / want an - y good thing.

Saint Andrew the Apostle's Day

The Introit *Formulary Tone VII*

(The Introit, or alternate, is the same as for Evangelists', Apostles', and Martyrs' Days, p. 148)

The Intervenient Chants *Formulary Tone VIII*

(The Gradual and the Alleluia, or the Alleluia, are the same as for Evangelists', Apostles', and Martyrs' Days, p. 150)

169

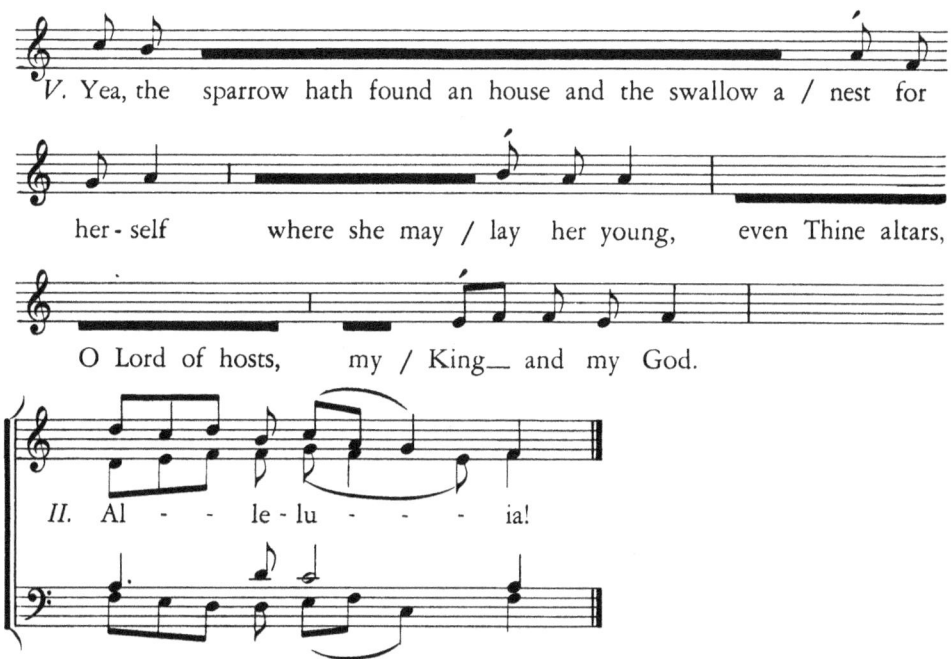

V. Yea, the sparrow hath found an house and the swallow a / nest for her-self where she may / lay her young, even Thine altars, O Lord of hosts, my / King and my God.

II. Al - - le - lu - - - ia!

The Mission Festival

The Introit   *Formulary Tone VIII*

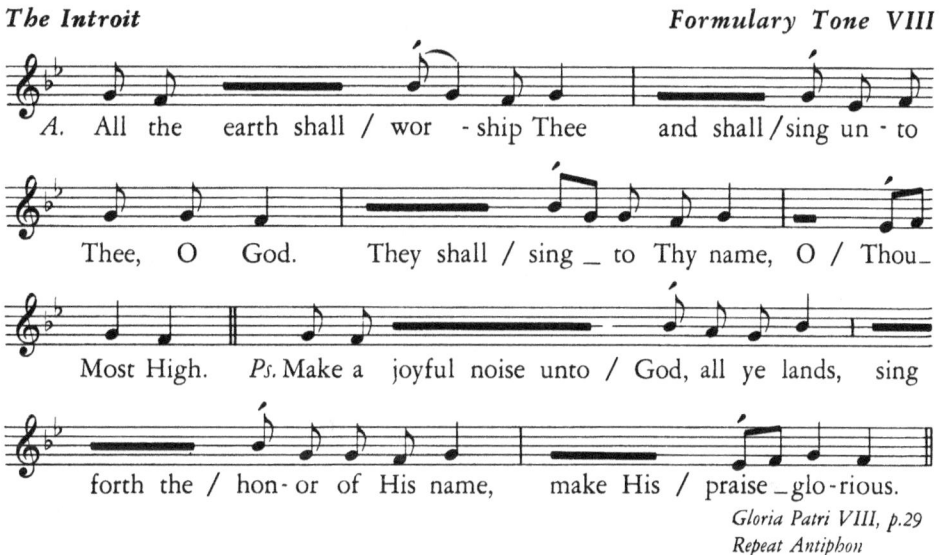

A. All the earth shall / wor-ship Thee and shall / sing un-to Thee, O God. They shall / sing to Thy name, O / Thou Most High. Ps. Make a joyful noise unto / God, all ye lands, sing forth the / hon-or of His name, make His / praise glo-rious.

Gloria Patri VIII, p.29
Repeat Antiphon

The Intervenient Chants   *Formulary Tone VII*

(The Gradual and the Alleluia are the same as for the First, Second, or Third Sunday after the Epiphany, p. 23)

www.ingramcontent.com/pod-product-compliance
Lightning Source LLC
Chambersburg PA
CBHW080919170426
43201CB00016B/2198